DR MARTIN RUFFLEY (BA, M.Litt, PhD) a multiple award-winning Master Chef, has travelled the world in his pursuit of culinary excellence.

In his role as a lecturer at GMIT he has trained numerous chefs that have competed at both a national and an international level with outstanding results. In 2020 he received the prestigious *President's Award for Teaching Excellence*.

More recently, his attention has focused on compiling a lifetime of recipes inspired by forty-years of travelling throughout the Middle East, USA, Australia, Thailand, Cambodia, Laos, Malaysia, China, Japan, Singapore, Vietnam, Continental Europe and Iceland, as well as staging at: Maaemo Restaurant, Oslo, Norway (3 Michelin Star); Hibiscus Restaurant, London, UK (2 Michelin Star); and ORA Restaurant, Helsinki, Finland (1 Michelin Star).

Dr Martin Ruffley

DR ANNA KING (BA, MA, PhD), is a writer with a specialisation in creative nonfiction, ethnography and the contemplative arts. She obtained a Doctorate in Philosophy (Ethnography), from NUI, Galway, for which her research was awarded a highly-esteemed three-year, full-time *Irish Research Council Scholarship* in 2010.

In addition to a life-time interest in mindful meditation, much of Anna's creative work is informed by a deep appreciation and love of nature. She grew up in a very remote area of Wiltshire, England, where her family grew most of their own food. When studying Zen Buddhism in the mid 1980s she was introduced to macrobiotic cooking and subsequently became hooked on the healing benefits of eating seasonal, natural foods. So much so that she went on to study, live and work at a number of organic farms in the UK and France that followed the philosophy of Mahatma Gandhi and Rudolf Steiner.

www.annaking.ie

Dr Anna King

Martin Ruffley & Anna King

REKINDLING THE FIRE

Food and the Journey of Life

AUSTIN MACAULEY PUBLISHERS™

LONDON • CAMBRIDGE • NEW YORK • SHARJAH

All food and nature photography © Julia Dunin – www.juliadunin.com

Landscape photography (pages 18 & 20) © Professor Chaosheng Zhang

Fire Photo (page 16) © Anna King

A CIP catalogue record for this title is available from the British Library.

ISBN 9781398447363 (Paperback)
ISBN 9781398447370 (Hardback)
ISBN 9781398447387 (ePub e-book)

www.austinmacauley.com

First Published 2022
Austin Macauley Publishers Ltd
1 Canada Square
Canary Wharf
London
E14 5AA

Dedication

We dedicate this book to Gemma and all those still struggling with addiction.

May the light of loving kindness illuminate your path, and the darkness of the night inspire your wildest dreams.

Acknowledgements

From Martin:

I would like to express my sincere gratitude to Jacinta Dalton (Head of Department in Culinary Arts at Galway International Hotel School) for her continuous support throughout this project. I would also like to thank Cormac Handy for his lasting friendship and much appreciated encouragement.

In particular, I would like to thank my family: without you this project would not have been possible. But, my deepest and sincerest gratitude goes to my wife, Bridie, for standing by me through the darker periods of my life. Your love, patience and support means everything to me. Thank you!

I would also like to thank Alcoholics Anonymous for their continued support, John Long for 'being there', Paul Hogan for listening to me and Robert Dagger for giving me a 'break'.

Lastly, I would like to take time to comment that working with my co-author Anna on this book has been an amazing experience. I would never have considered writing a book without her. She came to me a few years ago with the suggestion and a rough outline of how we may collaborate. The rest is history. Her ability to transform my stories and life-experiences into such beautiful prose took my breath away. It takes a lot of courage and trust to share the darkest moments of your life with another. I could not have gone through this creative process with anyone else.

Anna, you are a gifted writer, and a kind and patient friend. Thank you.

From Anna:

Working with Martin on this book has been one of the most rewarding creative experiences of my life. His energy and enthusiasm for cooking is contagious, and his recipes sublime. Compiling the recipes for this book has taken Martin many seasons of waiting for crops to mature, and sitting with each ingredient to sense the story that they have to tell. The time we spent tasting and styling recipes was really special. His attention to detail with every dish and the love that he has for every ingredient ignites a song in my soul, and poetry in my heart. It is pure magic.

Martin, I am honoured to have been part of this creative journey. Thank you for being so open about your experience of addiction, and for trusting me with such painful life-events.

Together we have transmuted the darkness of your past into a story of hope. To inspire, means to breathe life, and I am convinced that your story will bring inspiration to future generations and to families of those still suffering.

I would also like to thank my husband, George: your generous and creative insights reveal another layer to every experience. I have learnt so much from you and this book would not exist without your love and support.

Lastly, but by no means least, I would like to thank my son, Sean, for being the light of my life.

That you are so proud of this book being published means everything to me!

Joint acknowledgements:

We would like to thank Skipper and Claddagh man, Ciaran Oliver (and crew) for taking us out lobster fishing on Lovely Anne, a traditional Galway Hooker Boat. This breath-taking experience inspired our Irish chapter.

Another Claddagh acknowledgement: Thank you Mike Walsh and family for allowing us to use Katie's Claddagh Cottage for some of our content curation. Cooking winkles on an open fire and vintage hearth was the highlight of our recipe tasting experiences. Mike has also been a wonderful friend to Anna throughout the writing of this book, and his encouragement over the years will not be forgotten.

In addition, the images for this book are exceptional. Thank you, Julia Dunin. We are incredibly grateful for your creativity, curation and for being such a styling genius. Thank you SCCUL Sanctuary for providing such an amazing venue for Julia. It was the perfect light-filled space for our photoshoot.

Equally, we would like to thank Professor Chaosheng Zhang for his stunning photos of Galway.

We would like to express a special thank you to Conor Kenny, from Kenny's bookshop: We were honoured that you took the time to review our manuscript and offer such sage advice. Your review and subsequent support marked an important turning point for us, as it relieved our fears and boosted our confidence. For that we are extremely grateful!

Equally, a special thank you to Ian Scaramuzza for writing our foreword. We are extremely grateful that such a talented and popular chef would take time out from his busy schedule to read our book.

We would like to thank all of our local producers who provided fresh, seasonal and exceptional produce throughout the creation of this book. In particular, we would like to acknowledge: Galway Bay Seafoods, Burkes Fruit and Veg, Kelly's Oysters, Chef Paddy Philips for his foraged seaweed, Ernie's Fruit and Veg, Velvet Cloud, Mooncoin Beetroot, and Ballyhoura Mushrooms, Dela Restaurant, Beechlawn Organic Farm, NeighbourFood Oranmore and Thalli Foods.

Contents

Foreword

by Ian Scaramuzza

I was humbled and surprised when asked to write a foreword for a book at this stage in my career. Being a strange time in the world right now (during a pandemic), I couldn't refuse.

In particular, what really impresses me about this book is how inspirational it is. Every chapter is entirely different, with creative content to complement each dish, stunning photographs and eloquent descriptions of regional cuisine.

This book will inspire anyone who reads it to cook.

The recipes have easy to follow directions, providing home-cooks and chefs an opportunity to experiment with some really creative dishes that would normally be confined to professional kitchens. In addition, this book has another unique feature in that it is a deeply personal memoir of overcoming addiction through cooking, which is an issue close to the heart of many chefs worldwide. I have no doubt that this book will bring hope to individuals and families touched by the experience of addiction. In Martin's case he has gone on to travel the world, teach and use his personal experience of recovery to help others discover the wonderful potential inherent within the art of cuisine.

This book has a place in anyone's library.

Written by two authors, Anna King brings to life Martin's story through her experience of mindful meditation. Each chapter has beautifully descriptive prose that speaks directly to the reader about how cooking is more than food preparation, but also a journey of self-discovery and healing. For me this makes this book much more interesting to read than other cookbooks. Not only have I learnt some great recipes and techniques to add to my personal repertoire, but I thoroughly enjoyed the whole book, from beginning to end.

In the past few years I have cooked in Hong Kong, Singapore, Belgium, Amsterdam, Cayman Islands, and San Francisco, so I can relate to this book on a very personal level, as I believe that travel is an essential element of any chefs education, especially if they wish to get to the top of their profession. Martin's adventures around the globe certainly adds a special ingredient to each chapter.

I first met Martin in 2014 while I was head chef of Hibiscus restaurant in London, under Chef Claude Bosi (now of Bibendum). I was 28 years old at the time and it was my first head chef role, so it was an impactful time in my career. Hibiscus held two Michelin Stars, 5 AA Rosettes, it was a Member of Relais Chateaux, featured 9/10 in the Good Food Guide and was in the top 50 of the 50 Best Restaurants in the World, to name a few accolades.

We ran a fast-paced, highly pressurised kitchen, where everything was made from scratch, with 90% 'à la minute cooking' (there are not many kitchens working in this way). We had a lot of stagiaires coming through our kitchen, so we would only take someone for two weeks minimum. I was told by our PA that we had a college lecturer coming in for four weeks. I was a little nervous to be honest, knowing that Martin was a lecturer with a lot of work and life experience. I was also worried about the pressure our team was under.

Martin arrived early on his first day, which is always a good sign. To be honest, my first impression was that he wouldn't last the time, as he hadn't been working in a restaurant environment for quite some time due to his career change of becoming a lecturer. I was wrong! Martin worked as hard as anyone (working 16-17 hour days) moving with ease around the sections, as was planned for him. Everyone took to Martin's energy and enthusiastic attitude, and he quickly gained respect from the full team.

True to his word he worked the full four weeks. He brought a sense of calm to the less experienced cooks in the team. Having him around was a breath of fresh air. Needless to say we kept in contact after he finished, and he subsequently sent over one of his students, who also came with the same enthusiasm and talent, which shows Martin taught him well.

Martin's commitment to demystifying what would normally be perceived as complex dishes is testimony to his diligence and talent for teaching and imparting information. From this book you will learn how to create some amazing dishes that will transform a meal from the 'ordinary to the exceptional'.

I hope that you enjoy the journey that this book takes you on – I know I did – You will not be disappointed!

Ian is currently head chef at the 2 MICHELIN starred Melisse restaurant in Santa Barbara, California.

During his time as head chef at two-star Hibiscus, he was the recipient of the highly prestigious Roux Scholarship in 2015, and staged at three-star Benu with Cory Lee. Ian was also head chef at the ground-breaking MICHELIN Star In Situ restaurant at the Museum Of Modern Art, San Francisco.

Ian has worked in some of the best restaurants in the world, including: Andrew Fairlie's Gleneagles Hotel Restaurant, Albert Adria's Tickets, Restaurant Sat Bains, De Pastorale in Antwerp and the three-star De Leest in Holland. He also played a crucial role in a food waste collaboration (wastED) between Selfridges and Chef Dan Barber, and worked with Clare Smyth in developing her three-starred MICHELIN restaurant, Core in London.

Introduction

THIS IS NOT A CONVENTIONAL COOKBOOK

The recipes offer home-cooks, amateurs and seasoned chefs alike an opportunity to experiment with both new and old techniques, through easy to follow, concise instructions that will really 'up anyone's game' in the kitchen. You will learn how to create some magical dishes, as well as discover invaluable insider tips that will transform a meal from the ordinary to the exceptional.

However, there is more...

In addition to inspiring people to cook, *Rekindling the Fire* is a deeply personal memoir that demonstrates how cooking and the art of crafting recipes is a journey toward well-being, a process of salvation and an opportunity to create space to quieten the persistent echo of the chef's raging lived experience.

This beautifully crafted book offers hope to those still living with addiction. It demonstrates how a passion (such as cooking) can transform lives. Martin's life-journey proves that it is never too late to change, or to find the courage to take the first step toward a more life-enhancing, rewarding future.

All of the shadow-to-light-inspired recipes in this book are deeply textured experiences inspired by the process of addiction recovery, as well as Martin's travel overseas and his eventual return to the home-hearth to rekindle the fire of life after decades of alcoholism:

> The pain sears through my mind as I search for a crack in the darkness to reassure myself that I am alive. It's pitch black and there is only pain; aching, endless, screaming pain. The only sound is my heart pounding incessantly within my bruised-blue buckled ribs. Minutes, hours, days. All are one...
>
> I am now ready to return home.

For Martin creating and preparing a dish is a cathartic process of transmutation; a forty-year process of exorcising 'demons' and finding peace within the 'generous present moment' of being:*

Rekindling the Fire brings to life Martin's backstory of addiction through the prism of mindfulness. The first three chapters present a series of deeply layered recipes inspired by Martin's descent into alcoholism. The recipes in chapters four to seven are dishes celebrating cooking as a practice of self-discovery and healing.

As we move through the spaces in-between life and death, we cook

> Creating a menu is a mindful act of sacrificing the ego and giving way to 'flow'. It is about trusting and respecting the ingredients and where they come from; finding balance between action and non-action, and connecting with the eternal present.

---

*   'Generous present moment' quotation credited to neuroscientist Dr Joe Dispenza.

It is always about releasing the noise of life and putting aside the piercing silence of death.

It is about entering the spaces in-between.

In addition to sharing how cooking released Martin from the grips of addiction, this book introduces a new way of experiencing food:

> During my visit to Vietnam an unexpected encounter with the power of mindfulness unfolded. I had become fascinated by the family-run rice plantations that fanned in all directions from the outskirts of the city. One afternoon I spent some time watching a group of farmers tending their land. This was a seasoned way of life, where each grain of rice produced would hold the essence of previous generations who had gathered for centuries with the sole purpose of producing food that resonates with the heart of authenticity. I was taken by the sense of peace that emanated from their methodical, yet graceful movement. Nothing was forced or laboured. There was a sense that each movement flowed into the next, and that the art of farming was not separate from the crop being brought to life. The farmer and the land required each other: it was a continuous melody of energetic exchange, a deeply connected form of communication that had no spoken word. I had not witnessed anything like this before. It was as if the people, and this place, were intrinsically connected; the farmer and their land were a single patterned ecosystem.

> I was struck by the idea that food produced with such love was imbued with the energy of the caretaker, and as I witnessed this scene before me, I vowed to explore this elegant grace in my cooking. It was here in the fields near Hội An that I committed to a philosophy that became the foundation of my life's work – a way of cooking and living that inspired my every waking moment: to 'let food speak for itself'.

If the cultural encompasses the global, food embraces the local

Just like the seasons, food experiences change over time. Different trends come and go, some more dramatically than others. Over the last ten years Nordic countries have forged a completely new way of cooking that has challenged the very core of classical French style cuisine. The authors of this book believe that there is a new genre emerging, one that focuses on high quality ingredients, especially plants and locally sourced produce. This trend has a sustainable ethos (in response to the environmental crisis) and is culturally specific, meaning that it is place-based and inspired by the terroir. While these features are very much part of the new Nordic model (as detailed in Chapter VI), this book explores an additional feature: how to create the extraordinary out of the ordinary by becoming more familiar with each ingredient, and, in so doing, with oneself.

This is a philosophy and a way of life, not just a style of cooking. It is an invitation to experience food and its preparation as a way of thinking, feeling and being. It is about health and how action always has a reaction and it embraces a set of holistic principles that consider mindful cooking as a healing practice.

The recipes in this book are an opportunity for the reader to be part of this new food experience.

About the Recipes

The menus in this book came to life after a creative process of constant introspection that took place over many years, rather than simply sitting down and writing a list of complementary dishes. Each dish is deeply personal and as such there is an interplay between experience, times past, taste, culture, emotion and expression. These recipes are unlike those seen in other books because they leave room to create. They are guidelines (rather than recipes in the strictest sense) that provide you with an opportunity to express your personality and own interpretation. If you engage with an open mind, and follow the guiding principles, the results will differ from Martin's, but they will be quite amazing. All that matters when you experiment with these dishes is that you follow your heart:

> The rest will unfold in whatever way the ingredients *'speak to you'.* It is a process of creative alchemy and an opportunity to make the *extraordinary out of the ordinary.*

This book is written by two authors:

Dr Martin Ruffley speaks the language of food, and overcoming addiction. While his recipes have multiple layers of cultural complexity, there is a simplicity to his art – where 'food speaks for itself'. For Martin, cooking is about removing the veil of separation and delving deep into the essence of each ingredient. His dishes lift us from the mundane realm, elevating us toward an experience of food that is truly magical.

Dr Anna King brings to life Martin's life-journey with a creative nonfiction narrative that draws upon her extensive experience of mindful meditation and organic agriculture. They have come together to share food as art, the travels undertaken to reach the threshold of its creation, and the enormous healing potential inherent within the cooking experience.

Chapter I

A Menu From Home

Loss of Innocence

"I now know that it was the first drink that did the damage."

Fragments of my childhood are etched into the grey sky-scape of Galway City.

As I amble along the Long Walk the charcoal black cormorant's white shawl reflects a seasonal shift of light, and the heron, with its steely grey stare and awkward gait, languishes in sight of the Spanish Arch.

An unnatural coldness dampens my spirit just as the impenetrable sea-drenched mist releases its shroud.

I pause.

Poisoned shadows lurk nearby...

I look to *Claddagh!*

The scent of wood-smoke, the salted dew
Crafted boats against a backdrop of blue

And as a leaf falls down with patterned sound

A westerly wind and soft morning light
Takes me back to that cursed night

When the city lost its muted tones
and those delicate greys turned into a bright red blaze.

And so it all began, all those years ago.

The mark of the darkened moon was cast upon my brow, just as I reached for that wretched bottle.

Calling the Soul Back Home:

A sense of place, the loss of innocence and a journey of self-reflection inspire this menu, as well as Claddagh, where I spent much of my childhood.

The Claddagh is an ancient fishing village, nestled on the edge of Galway City. It dates back to the 7th Century and is famous for *Galway Hookers* (traditional wooden boats) and the Claddagh ring, designed by renowned goldsmith, Richard Joyce, circa 1700. The Claddagh fishermen and their wives lived in rows of white-washed thatched cottages. They were a distinct community with their own culture, norms and laws (they even had their own *King of Claddagh)*. This close-knit community lost much of its identity in the 1930s when the Galway City Council knocked down all their houses (due to a severe case of TB and inadequate sanitation). My mother is a Claddagh woman, and the energy and spirit of this unique community runs through the entirety of this menu.

I have a deep personal connection to each dish in this chapter.

Whether it's sourcing produce, preparing ingredients or cooking, every step of the experience is about '*bringing my soul back home'* to the innocence of my childhood.

But, as I share these stories with you, I am conscious of the fragility of my memories, as they are laced with dark tales of violence, pubs and being silenced in a masculine world of intolerance and foreboding.

The pain of such suffocation is tempered now by cooking, whereby my senses take me on a journey. Whether it's the smell of seaweed or the scent of meat cooking on a grill; every aspect of my food experience alludes to community, family and a sense of belonging.

Cooking has enabled me to transmute the disease that penetrated my soul. It has re-introduced me to my past through the eyes of art, colour, texture, touch and most importantly, the love – of food.

The act of cooking these dishes represents constraint, something that I lost once I took that first drink. Later on in life, through cooking and the support of friends and family, I found the restraint necessary to stop drinking and I was able to completely turn my life around.

It's difficult to describe the power that alcohol once had over me. I cannot count the times that I 'fell off the wagon'. The compulsion (craving) would descend, and I succumbed. I found myself before the courts, being admitted to hospital. I lost my job and my family.

I was plagued constantly with guilt and yet, I found myself back in that vicious circle of madness, chaos, violence and sickness. I was totally baffled by how this happened! At times, I even protested my innocence!

Ultimately, I never intended to do the things that I have done; but, once I took a drink everything went out of the window and all that mattered was the next drink.

Today, cooking grounds me in the here and now. It liberates me from the cage of doubt, remorse and self-hate. I now have time to remember the positive aspects of my baptism from childhood to adulthood. It is not denial. It is more about making a choice to allow life to enter into my present, by making peace with my past.

I haven't forgotten, I have just learnt to let go!

A Menu from Home

Loss of Innocence

Periwinkles with Fermented Potato Cakes

Smoked, Roasted Hen of the Wood,
with Mushroom Seaweed Broth

Salted Mackerel, Potato, Ramsons and Pickled Gooseberries

Connemara Mountain Lamb, with Beetroot

Gorse Flower and Sugar Kelp Cream

This menu invites you to sit mindfully with the ingredients before
cooking:

Savour the colours, texture and tones.

If you can source the ingredients locally, then visit where they come from.

Smell the scent of salt from the sea air and feel the seaweed beneath
your feet.

Enjoy the mud of earthy potato skins and the heady woodland glades of
garlic.

Be in the moment.

Periwinkles with Fermented Potato Cakes

Long before the term foraging became trendy, I used to help my father (Tommy) to pick periwinkles, which he had done with his father before him. As with the weeding, I didn't enjoy it as it was often cold, wet and backbreaking. The winkles would be placed into canvas bags, tied, and left for the tide to come over them. At the following low tide, we would continue to forage and add to the bag. When we had the required amount, they would be collected and my Dad was paid by the weight. This additional income was important in supporting a very large family (11 in total).

We always brought some of the forage home and my Mother would cook them, served with potatoes and vinegar.

I remember one cold morning on Ballyloughane beach. Prior to starting work, my Dad asked me to leave the tea and sandwiches in a safe place. Whilst doing so, I slipped on some seaweed and the flask of tea hit a rock.

For the next two hours I was dreading the tea break!

When it came around, my 'heart was in my mouth,' as Dad opened the sandwiches. He then proceeded to open the flask. As he started to pour the tea, all the shattered silver lining came out into the cup.

To say he was annoyed is an understatement!

I ran all the way home.

By the time he got back, he had calmed down.

Fifty years later, my younger brother continues to pick winkles.

This recipe is a rendition of my mother's recipe with kombucha replacing the vinegar, bringing a subtle acidity to the dish and the fermented potato cakes instead of boiled potatoes.

Serves 4

Live Periwinkles 2.5kg
Onion 200g
Carrot 50g
Celery 20g
Apple Kombucha 15ml
Mussel Stock 100ml
Rapeseed Oil 1 teaspoon
Butter 10g

1. Wash winkles in plenty of cold water.
2. Soak in a little seawater for 20–30 minutes. Drain.
3. Add a dash of rapeseed oil to a pan. Add finely diced onion, carrot and celery. Cook until translucent.
4. Add winkles, mussel stock and apple kombucha.
5. Cook winkles for approximately 3 to 4 minutes.
6. Remove winkles from their shells, making sure to remove the hard foot at the top end.
7. Reheat the vegetables and cooking liquor, add winkles. Whisk in the butter.

To Serve: Place winkles onto fermented potato cakes.

Fermented Potato

New Potatoes 1kg
Achill Sea Salt 20g (2%)
Still Water, as required

1. Cook potatoes in boiling salted water until cooked.
2. Allow to cool and peel.
3. Place a large Kilner jar onto weighing scales and set to zero.
4. Place potatoes into the jar and cover with still water.
5. Calculate total weight, add 2% sea salt and cover with a lid.
6. Allow to ferment in a dark place (entirely away from sunlight) at room temperature for 10–12 days.
7. If not for immediate use, store in the refrigerator for up to 3 months.

Serves 4

New Potatoes 1kg
Butter (Cuinneog) 100g
Organic Plain Flour 100g
Achill Sea Salt 10g
Diced Fermented Potato 350g

1. Bake the washed potatoes in a hot oven until cooked.
2. Peel and pass the potatoes through a ricer (or sieve into a clean bowl).
3. Add flour (holding back some for dusting), melted butter (cooled), and add salt to taste.
4. Add diced fermented potato.
5. Scale into 50-gram pieces.
6. Place between 2 pieces of parchment or silicone paper to shape.
7. Cook on a hot, dry skillet or pan for 2 minutes on each side.

Smoked Roasted Hen of the Wood with Mushroom and Seaweed Broth

The mushroom and seaweed dish is about bringing the woods and the sea together.

Galway has an unusual landscape. While some describe it as stunning, there is a sound and tone to our land that resonates hardship.

This howling land of ours is unforgiving:

The brittle breaking of the hawthorn bough drowns out the screaming wind as it punishes the rattling iron-gate, banging for forgiveness in the distance.

Our windswept winter land stirs a restlessness that aches for attention.

And yet, such lost moments of ghostly turmoil give way to a summer's charm and, almost in a flicker, the trickling spring water from the mountains arrests the tears of the sea and there is suddenly quietness in the land.

A union of burnt umber, silica green grey and flecks of dancing chestnut brown.

Serves 4

Hen of the Woods Mushrooms 2

Achill Island Sea Salt (to season)

Dried Mushrooms 200g

Water 300ml

Kombu 50g

Rapeseed Oil – a dash

You will need a muslin cloth

1. Thoroughly clean the hen of the woods mushrooms with a brush or cloth.
2. Heat the water and pour over the dried mushroom and kombu.
3. Leave to infuse for one hour.
4. Season the mushrooms with sea salt and drizzle over some rapeseed oil.
5. Lightly smoke for 1–2 hours.
6. Roast the mushrooms in a hot oven 180°C for 5–7 minutes.
7. Strain the mushroom and seaweed infusion through a muslin cloth.
8. Gently heat the broth and check for seasoning.

To Serve: Place roasted mushrooms in a serving bowl and pour in the broth.

Note: To smoke the mushrooms take a deep tray and add a layer of hay, apple, cherry or chicory wood-chips. Ignite and quench, then cover with a layer of tin foil and place your mushrooms on top. Seal with cling film and another layer of tin foil to keep the smoke inside. This technique can also be done with a biscuit tin.

Salted Mackerel, Potatoes, Ramson and Pickled Gooseberries

The salted mackerel dish is dedicated to my father's old school pal, Eamonn McDonagh, and my mother-in-law, Máire Griffin.

Eamonn was a fisherman who looked after my family by giving us fish, a mainstay in our house.

Being the eldest, I would go down to the docks every Thursday evening when the boats came in and Mr McDonagh would give me a bag of fish to bring home.

Mackerel are in season around May and peak in July and August when shoals come in with the warm sea temperature. Salted fish, mackerel and herring have been salted on the west coast of Ireland for centuries as a means of preserving. Traditionally, the fish was salted, dried and then added to boiling potatoes near the end of cooking. On the Aran Islands they continue the old tradition of eating salted Ling and potatoes on Christmas Eve.

This dish is my interpretation of fish and potatoes, with the addition of gooseberries to cut through the richness of the fish and wild garlic for flavour.

I have used poitín in this dish, a favourite of my mother-in-law. Poitín is an illegal homemade moonshine made with fermented potatoes and malted barley. Occasionally, crab-apples were also added. The name comes from the pot in which it was made. Máire used to cook herrings by pouring poitín over them and setting them on fire. This is very much in line with contemporary cooks using blowtorches. Both my father and mother-in-law came from Connemara, where poitín was not only enjoyed as a drink, but also used medicinally to ease sore joints, teething babies and much more. When my daughter Olivia was teething Máire used to rub poitín onto her gums.

Serves 4

Mackerel 4 x 300g fillets
Achill Island Sea Salt 2g
New Potatoes 400g
Butter 50g
Wild Garlic Ramsons 50g
Pickled Gooseberries 10g
Rapeseed Oil 10ml
Poitín – a dash
Garum – a little

1. Fillet the mackerel, remove pin bones, and pat dry with kitchen paper.

2. Salt fish, cover with cling film and refrigerate for 45 minutes.

3. Wash and cook potatoes in boiling salted water until cooked.

4. Rinse salt from fish, pat dry and score the skin.

5. Pan fry mackerel in a hot pan with rapeseed oil skin side down. As soon as it takes on colour turn over, flame with poitín, lightly brush over with garum and finish cooking. The fish can also be grilled or blow-torched.

To Serve: Place mackerel onto a plate and garnish with gooseberries, flowers and ramsons. Drizzle over with rapeseed oil. Serve buttered potatoes on the side.

Connemara Mountain Lamb with Beetroot

This lamb dish represents my time working as a 'messenger' boy for Colleran's butchers on Mainguard Street, where I would deliver the meat orders all over the city on an old bicycle. Messenger is an old Irish saying that means to 'get the messages'. It refers to groceries. My mother was delighted with me, since Mr Colleran was a very kind and generous man: on a Saturday evening when work was all done, and in addition to my wage, he would give me a big parcel of meat to bring home.

It warms my heart to see that this family butcher is still open for business today.

Serves 4

Lamb Loin 800g
Lamb Breast 1kg
Lamb Bones 1kg
Chicken Stock 1500ml
Butter 200g
Wild Garlic 10g
Lemon Thyme, a few sprigs
Potatoes 500g
Baby Beetroots 400g
Brine (see recipe below)

1. Brine the lamb breast overnight and store in the refrigerator.
2. Remove from the brine and dry with kitchen paper. Season and slow cook in the oven for five to six hours at 160°C, until it is wonderfully tender (retain some of the fat).
3. Allow to cool and shred the meat by hand.
4. Thinly slice the peeled potatoes (a mandolin is very useful).
5. Lightly butter a roasting dish and line with parchment paper.
6. Start with a layer of seasoned sliced potatoes and alternate with cooked shredded lamb meat, finishing with a layer of potato.
7. Cover with more parchment paper and cook in a hot oven 180°C for 45 minutes, or until the potatoes are cooked.
8. Place a heavy tray/plate on top to compress and chill in the refrigerator overnight.
9. Make the lamb jus.
10. Wash beets, season, wrap in tinfoil and bake for 25 minutes and put aside.
11. Turn potato and lamb terrine onto a chopping board.
12. Cut into 10cm long and 3cm wide portions.
13. Season lamb loin and sear on a hot pan until nicely browned.
14. Roast for 20 minutes and rest for 15 minutes in a warm place.
15. While your lamb is resting, pan fry the potato and lamb terrine on both sides to golden brown.

16. Finish potato and lamb terrine and the beets in the same oven.

17. Heat the lamb jus (see below) and add any juice from the rested loin.

To Serve: Place potato and lamb terrine on the plate. Add carved loin, baby beetroot and pour over sauce. Garnish with wild garlic.

Brine

Sea Salt 300g
Brown Sugar 120g
Pink Curing Salt
2 teaspoons
Sprig of Rosemary
Garlic Cloves (crushed) 3
Juniper Berries 6
Star Anise 2
Water 4 litres

1. Place all the ingredients into a non-reactive pan. Add cold water.

2. Bring to the boil, ensuring that both the salt and sugar have dissolved.

3. Allow to cool.

4. Add your lamb to the brine, cover with cling film and store for 2 to 3 days in the refrigerator

5. Rinse in cold water. Dry, cover and chill for another 4 hours and use as required.

Lamb Jus

Lamb Bones 1kg
Chicken Stock 2000 ml
(see page 142)
Shallots 3
Butter 5g

1. Brown bones in a hot oven.

2. Cut shallots in half with skins on and brown in a hot pan.

3. Place bones and shallots into a pan, add chicken stock and bring to the boil.

4. Simmer gently for 45 minutes, skimming any impurities that rise to the surface.

5. Strain and reduce by half.

6. Remove from heat, whisk in some butter, check for seasoning and serve.

Gorse Flower and Sugar Kelp Cream

Finally, the dessert invokes memories of gathering seaweed for our garden (another chore that I disliked immensely).

Once again, this dish emphasises the element of wood, as well representing the essence of our rugged wild Atlantic coastline.

Gorse is one of the most prolific features of our seascape. Its vibrant golden-yellow flowers are often associated with the Celtic god of light, *Lugh* (god of the sun and summer). As a symbol of love, fertility and protection, gorse featured in the ancient Celtic feast of Bealtaine, which is celebrated on May Day. The flowers are traditionally gathered at dawn and placed on door-posts to ward off evil. This shrub has a high oil content, which would have been useful to light the Bealtaine fire.

Gorse will flower continually all year, although it is particularly striking in the spring, as its bright colour heralds a new season. Its flowers are edible and can be made into infusions. They have a slight coconut and almond note. The buds can be salted and then pickled and used like capers.

Ode to the land of gorse: a love lost in transience

Breaking through the indigo night sky the cadmium yellow gorse flower arrives unannounced to herald the arrival of spring. She holds no subtle secrets as she gazes out across the cold tin-white dew washed up on the scattered shoreline.

A cacophony of gulls watch with jilted stares, as the gorse flower commands the attention of the sun to warm her prickly arrogance in preparation for final combat with the last shadow of winter. And, as the evening light rests upon the glazed grey Atlantic swirl, tails of sea kelp creep toward the stunted shaly-shore.

Gorse and kelp behold each other's worth and, just for a moment, they rest in each other's splendour.

As dusk greets darkness with notes of woody almond nectar, kelp now dances alone amidst salt crystals of luminous light. All that remains are pebbles battling for expression against rock, earth, stone and sand.

Serves 4

Cream 400ml
Milk 100ml
Carrageen Moss 10g
Sugar Kelp 10g
Gorse Flowers 350g
Gorse Sprigs 75g
Egg Yolks 2
Caster Sugar 50g
Water 75ml

1. Make stock syrup with 30g of the sugar, water, gorse twigs and flowers.

2. Cut sugar kelp into small pieces and poach in stock syrup for 2 hours.

3. Whisk the remaining 20g of sugar and egg yolk to ribbon stage and pour in the scalded cream and milk.

4. Cook over low heat until slightly thickened.

5. Add washed carrageen moss & gorse flowers and infuse for 30 minutes.

6. Strain and add the pieces of sugar kelp.

7. Pour into a bowl (or cocktail glass) and refrigerate to set.

To Serve: Garnish with gorse flowers.

REKINDLING THE FIRE

Chapter II

Levant Menu

Manhood

This chapter is inspired by the Middle East, my transition into adulthood, as well as a colleague, Denis Westman, who was an excellent veteran of field cookery. He was a huge inspiration to me!

The menu is dedicated to the people of Lebanon, where I served with the *United Nations Interim Force in Lebanon* (UNIFIL) in 1980, 1983, 1985 and 1986. Our assignment was peace-keeping and distributing humanitarian aid. Although most of my time was spent in South Lebanon, I had the privilege of visiting Jordan, Israel and Damascus.[1]

When I set off on my travels I was a young man full of passion, adventure and adrenaline. As is often the case with youth, I yearned to discover far off lands and new horizons from which to test my brittle confidence.

I have a deep respect and love for the Lebanese people. Their warmth and hospitality during my stay was exceptional, especially given the hardship that they continually endured. Such turbulent, yet fond recollections are timeless, brought to life in the present-day by the scent of fresh thyme, mint, roasted sesame seeds, sumac and salt. When I use these ingredients Lebanon speaks to me. It is true to say that the authenticity of the people that I met during my stay has shaped the quality and character of the chef that I am today.

The aura of this region is imbued in these dishes and I hope that you too feel inspired to create a dish that resonates with the magic of this special place.

Enjoy!

---

1 The ancient lands of Israel, Jordan, Lebanon and parts of Syria are known as the Levant ('rising' in French).

Levant Menu

Manhood

Tabbouleh

Baba Ganoush

Manoushi

Grilled Spiced Chicken

Watermelon and Rosewater with Barzak

This menu is ideal for sharing.

It stimulates a sense of belonging and conviviality and invites us to sit in the presence of our authentic self and to trust the process of nature's unfolding natural beauty.

Beirut 1980: *I went to war-torn Lebanon as a young man and came home a very different person:*

The smell of rubber tyres against the dust of burnt sienna left a metallic taste in my dry mouth. I wasn't sure whether the salty sweat condensed upon my brow was real or imagined. This place was nothing like anything I had experienced in Ireland, and yet – it was deeply familiar.

The breathtaking backdrop of Mount Hermon cradled our fears and supervised our presence, as we carved our way on convoy along the coastal road from Beirut to Sidon and Tyre en route for the southern village of Haddatha.[2]

The road meandered through aromatic, uplifting orange blossom groves and sweet banana plantations that framed the incandescent cobalt Mediterranean ocean, which stretched as far as the eye could see. These exceptionally expansive vistas played tricks on my mind, as they were in stark contrast to the constellations of devastation that would incessantly puncture seeming moments of reprieve. Some of these images changed fast, others slow. And, as soporific moans and oil-stained glares bounced off the sun's piercing arrogance, I longed for shade. Darkness.

When the slate blue-grey night shadows eventually sliced through the day's heat, the sound of deafening shrapnel kept us awake. The intolerable scent of burning leather, tar and tobacco stirred a repulsion and thirst that knew no bounds. While it took many years for the fullness of these experiences to take hold of my fragile ego, it is true to say that these war-torn landscapes of Lebanon seared into my soul from the very minute I arrived.

As we move through the spaces in-between life and death, we cook!

Working as a chef is often characterised as operating in a pressurised, hot and demanding environment.

Being a chef working in a war zone is a different kettle of fish altogether. It's hard to describe what it's like to cook in a hostile environment…that is, unless you have been there.

You cannot compare it to working in a professional kitchen. Perhaps the biggest difference is that you are armed, which means that you have your weapon with you at all times. You are often working in less than ideal conditions, limited equipment, space, extreme heat, little or no ventilation, dealing with scorpions, snakes, or working with field cookers and then coming under fire. Occasionally, the lines would be closed, largely due to incidents or shelling, and we would have to use the dreaded dry rations.

On my third and final tour of duty (1985-6) I was based at our HQ, an observation post (619 Charlie) overlooking the Israeli buffer zone (a strip of Lebanon that the *Israeli Defense Forces* (IDF) partitioned). I remember we came under shellfire and we were in the bunker on groundhog. Groundhog is the term used to take cover in the bunker when you come under heavy fire. On this occasion, I was preparing dinner when the order to groundhog came. I was no sooner in the bunker than I realised that I had left the potatoes on the stove. I quickly dashed to the kitchen, strained the spuds and returned to the bunker. My concern at the time was to save the potatoes, not realising that it could have proved fatal.

It was just another day cooking in a hostile environment and it was in these smoke-filled makeshift kitchens that I discovered my salvation, even before I needed it. As I moved from place to place an ill-fated stare replaced my youthful glee.

A torrential anger began to smoulder, softened to this day only by cooking.

---

2 Mt. Hermon is the highest mountain in the region with peaks ranging from 7,336 ft to 9,232 ft. Its melting snow feed the Jordan and the Sea of Galilee.

Tabbouleh

Tabbouleh is a traditional salad served in the Levant. It consists of finely chopped parsley, tomato, spring onion, mint, bulgur wheat, and seasoned with lemon juice and olive oil.

The first time that I ate tabbouleh was in 1980 while serving with the United Nations Interim Force in Lebanon (UNIFIL). Indeed, it was the first time that I saw an aubergine growing in a field and olive oil being used on food. My only previous experience of olive oil was when my mother put it into my ears to remove wax. Forty years later baba ganoush, tabbouleh and hummus are hugely popular dishes all over the world.

Serves 4

Water 50ml
Bulgur Wheat 100g
Ripe Tomatoes 350g
Spring Onions 6
Juice of 2 Lemons
Parsley (Flat Leaf) 200g
Mint 50g
Olive Oil 80ml
Cucumber 50g (optional)

1. Rinse the bulgur wheat in cold water. Drain well and transfer to a suitable bowl and pour boiling water over. Cover with cling film.

2. Fluff up with a fork after 10 minutes. The short soaking time ensures a crunchy bulgur.

3. Finely chop the tomatoes, spring onions, parsley and mint (do not chop the herbs too fine as all the flavour will leech out onto to chopping board).

4. Add the above ingredients to the bulgur with the lemon juice and olive oil.

5. Check for seasoning.

To Serve: Transfer to a large bowl and drizzle over with olive oil.

Baba Ganoush

Serves 4

Aubergine 1
Garlic Cloves 1
Tahini Paste 2 tablespoons
Juice of 1 Lemon
Sea Salt to season
Olive Oil – a good drizzle

1. Blacken the aubergine on a hot plancha, or roast in a hot oven until soft for 25 to 30 minutes.

2. Remove the charred skin and seeds.

3. Drain the aubergine flesh in a colander for at least 20 minutes. It is important to remove the moisture.

4. Transfer garlic cloves and sea salt into a pestle and mortar and pound to a purée.

5. Add the aubergine and tahini paste and pound to a smooth paste.

6. Add lemon juice and check for seasoning.

To Serve: Transfer to a suitable dish and garnish with olive oil and chopped parsley. You can also add pomegranate seeds.

Note: You can also use a food processor/blender. However, using a pestle and mortar is more authentic. It is important to get the right balance of smokiness, acidity, garlic and tahini right. You can adjust the above amounts to suit your own taste.

Manoushi

Manoushi is a Lebanese/Syrian style flat-bread, which is much loved throughout the Middle East. It is similar to a pizza, but with a softer texture. During the cooking process an air pocket is created, that can be filled with almost anything. The most popular filling among Irish troops serving in Lebanon was egg and chips, more commonly known as "double double".

I have vivid memories of observing a local woman in the village of Baraachit making and cooking the bread on a Saj (a dome-shaped metal grill) over a fire of dried camel dung.

In Lebanon, the Manoushi is usually spiced with Za'atar, a wild thyme that grows all over the hills. It is blended with sumac, sesame seeds and salt (it can also be purchased in specialist grocery stores).

To eat za'atar is to remember the land from which the herb was gathered.

Flour (Plain) 350g
Dried Yeast 1 teaspoon
Salt – a good pinch
Sugar – a good pinch
Water (tepid) 175-200 ml
Olive Oil – a dash

1. In a mixing machine using a dough hook, add the flour, yeast and salt.

2. Dissolve the sugar in water and add it to the dry ingredients.

3. Mix the dough until you achieve a sticky texture. Transfer to a floured surface.

4. Add the olive oil and knead until you have a smooth dough.

5. Transfer to a lightly oiled bowl and prove until double in size (approximately 2–3 hours).

6. Knock back and scale into 10 portions. Cover with a cloth and rest for 15 minutes.

7. Roll each portion into a round to about 15 to 18 cm in diameter

8. Bake in a hot oven, preferably on a hot baking stone until it blisters and takes on a little colour (1–2 minutes).

9. Wrap in a clean cloth to keep warm while you are baking the rest of them.

To Serve: Place on a large flat dish or board.

Grilled Spiced Chicken

The Lebanese are a very hospitable people and would often welcome us into their homes. This recipe is a take on a dish that I had in the village of As Sultaniyah, just north of Tibnine, where we were treated to an excellent lunch of chicken cooked on a charcoal grill with salad, followed by a glass of chai on the veranda.

Set against the back drop of the Crusader Castle and the Wadi below, this was one of my most enjoyable food experiences. It was about the people, as much as the food, and as I write, I long to go back there again.

Serves 4

Chicken (furuj) Thighs 12
Lemons, Juice and Zest 2
Olive Oil 120ml
Garlic Cloves 4
Smoked Paprika
2 teaspoons
Cumin Seeds 5g
Coriander Seeds 5g
10 Cardamom Pods
(Green)
Chilli Powder 1 teaspoon
Sea Salt 1 to 2 teaspoons
Greek/Plain Yogurt 300g

1. Toast the coriander and cumin seed on a dry pan to release the oils and pass through a spice grinder. Alternatively, pound in a pestle and mortar.

2. Grate and juice the 2 lemons.

3. Transfer the chicken pieces into a bowl (or a zip lock bag) with the lemon juice, lemon rind, olive oil and all the dry ingredients.

4. Mix well and refrigerate overnight.

5. To cook: remove the chicken from the refrigerator at least 30 minutes before cooking. The chicken pieces can be skewered and grilled on a BBQ, or can be transferred to a suitable dish and roasted in a hot oven for 25 to 30 minutes.

To Serve: Drizzle with yogurt and serve with manoushi bread.

Note: Chicken breast can also be used. Butterfly the chicken breast and bat it out, then marinade (as above). This will cook on a grill in 8 to 10 minutes.

Watermelon and Rosewater Ice with Barazek

This dish is inspired by the generous nature of the locals, who so kindly gave us watermelon to quench the thirst from the hot summer sun while on checkpoint duty at Tibnine Bridge. To this day, I have never tasted a watermelon as sweet.

And, of course barazeks are wonderful biscuits that are found all over Lebanon. They are utterly delicious.

Serves 4

Watermelon 1kg
Caster Sugar 150g
Glucose 50g
Rosewater – a dash
Lemon Juice of 2
Watermelon Seeds 5g

1. Chop the watermelon and put the seeds aside.
2. Blitz the watermelon to a purée.
3. Add sugar to a pan with glucose and heat gently until dissolved.
4. Cool down and add the watermelon purée.
5. Add rosewater and lemon juice to taste.
6. Churn in an ice-cream machine or place into a container and cover with a lid and freeze.

To Serve: Transfer into a cocktail glass or bowl, sprinkle with watermelon seeds and serve with barazeks (see next recipe).

Rosewater can be purchased in any Middle-Eastern store.

Barazek Sesame and Pistachio Biscuits

Yield: 20 to 25 biscuits

Brown Sugar 20g
Icing Sugar 20g
Butter (unsalted) 75g
Egg 1 (medium)
Vanilla Essence – a few drops
Flour 100g
Pistachio Nuts 20g
Sesame Seeds 20g

1. Cream the butter, icing sugar and brown sugar together until light and fluffy.
2. Add vanilla essence and slowly add the beaten egg and then the flour.
3. Scale into small pieces and mould with your hand into little balls.
4. Shape into discs 1cm thick.
5. Press one side of the biscuit into sesame seeds and the other side onto the finely chopped pistachios.
6. Bake for 8 to 10 minutes in a hot oven 180°C.
7. Transfer to a wire rack to cool and serve.

To Serve: As an accompaniment to the watermelon dish.

Chapter III

No Place | No One

Rather than being inspired by a specific country, these recipes represent a period of my life when my alcoholism was totally out of control.

No Place | No One

Damper
(Also known as bush bread, which is made by crushing a variety
of roots & seeds)

Sea Snails and Lardo with Beach Herbs

Beef with Horseradish and Waffles

Salad of Organic Vegetables

Apple Leather with Aromatic Flowers

"The sweet scent of your fruit rests upon the pillow of my dreams."

This menu is a tribute to interconnectedness, togetherness and
companionship. It is an invitation for you to cook and rejoice in the
reality that we all need each other.

Gatherer of Night Shadows

As the mirror shattered
into a thousand experiences
the hours passed
into days
weeks
months.

And, then my soul
began to drift
to far off places,
toward distant voices,
lonely shadows.

During these wretched years my body constantly ached with heat, yet my mind was frozen like ice. I feared what would happen if I released all the jagged thoughts from the cage of my darkness.

Everyday waves of nausea retched through my will to stay awake. I was constantly tired yet, sleep, when it came, was no more than an incessant scream.

I was interested in no-one, nothing, except the next drink.

It was poetry in motion.
Repetitive ugly forceful stanzas that cursed every wretched moment.
There was no release from its power.
The rhythm
of each verse
crucified my reckless behaviour,
and plagued all attempts at self-justified reason.
This was the loud verse of
denial
loathing
and loss.

I attempted to dull the ache with constant travelling to far off places:

As the lost years went by I became estranged from my family. I ended up couch surfing, until people had had enough. By now even the hard core had given me the 'slip'. I was unreliable and unemployable! I couldn't fight the craving for drink. From here on in, everything went south. I became homeless, sleeping in a derelict house...

Loneliness, hopelessness, guilt, remorse: the self-loathing and alienation became too much to bear, as the drink was no longer blocking this stuff out.

I couldn't see a life with or without drink!

In 2000 I went to Australia to change my life. I thought foolishly that travelling to a far off distant land would provide a fresh start. It didn't last long. Within a short space of time I was back drinking again. All that I had done was change location. The difference was that now I was in the 'early house' wearing shorts and a T-shirt. The feelings were the same.

Damper

It was Johnny Gilbert (a native Australian) who showed me how to make damper, as well as educate me on aboriginal culture. He was a kitchen porter in a place that I worked in Melbourne. Johnny and his cousin (whose name I cannot recall) lived in Dandenong. They brought me out into the bush for a weekend, where I had the opportunity to witness their foraging and cooking skills (bush tucker).

We ate goanna lizard and murang damper, yam daisies and witchetty grubs, washed down with copious amounts of Victorian Bitter (VB).

Damper is a metaphor for my descent into madness and chaos.

Serves 4

Self-raising Flour 250g
Salt – a pinch
Butter 20g
Milk 170g
Dandelion root 1g (finely chopped)
Pumpkin, sunflower, flax seeds 1g

1. Rub the butter into the flour, add dandelion root, seeds, salt and milk and mix to a soft dough.
2. Transfer the damper into a greased billycan or mess tin.
3. Place under the hot embers (never in the fire), or bake in a hot oven 180°C for 25 minutes approx.
4. Cook for 20 to 30 minutes until it is crisp on the outside and fluffy inside.

To Serve: Break into four portions and serve with plenty of butter.

Sea Snails with Lardo and Beach Herbs

In 2010 I made the pilgrimage to the village of Colonnata in the Apuan Alps, where the famous Lardo Di Colonnata is made.

Colonnata is part of the Comune Massa-Carrara, an ancient settlement in Tuscany that dates back to Roman times. It is famous for both its marble and lardo. Much of the marble used for many of the sculptures and buildings in Florence, Siena and Pisa is thought to have originated from this far off mountain range.

Getting to this hinterland of historical significance was a serious endeavour.

We followed the winding, withered, off-the-beaten tracks that passed through the villages of Vezzala and Bedizzano.

Nestled between the mountains of Maggiore, Spallone and Sagro, Colonnata is surrounded by enormous quarries, including the Gioia Pit, which produces some of the most sought-after marble in the world.

I was mesmerised by the region's dramatic mountain-scape. It was an arresting relief of contrasts; a patchwork of etched beech and horse chestnut trees interrupted by glaring cubes of distant white marble. Seduced by dancing shadows of misty white light, I became transfixed by a summit that pierced through the classic Tuscan skyline. The aggressively carved cold stone and the severity of its presence, reminded me of my own inner journey: a raging alcoholic navigating the elements in search of the alchemy that food and the art of cooking could elicit.

The landscape of Colonnata is other-worldly and yet, I related to its foreboding ghost-like presence. I felt the scars of damnation that were ripped into the mountainside. It was like a menacing dreamscape that rebounds every time you attempt to push it away. Just like alcohol.

Colonnata is a sculptured expression of human compulsion. Its creaking crevices represent the multiple layers of psychological complexity embedded within the justification for lives torn asunder by the creation of art, slavery, loss and a world made beautiful by the grit and tears of human hands and nature's generosity.

It is a story of both purity and of human survival.

In Colonnata the lardo is traditionally cured in a marble basin with a mixture of salt, pepper, rosemary and garlic. Sometimes, cloves or nutmeg, as well as sage, star anise, oregano, coriander or even cinnamon can be added to the symphony. Covered in heavy marble 'blankets', the lard is cured at room temperature for a minimum of six months, while being cared for by artisan butchers.

My love of lardo is intrinsically linked to the experience of the mountains of Colonnata, as well as its surprising sweet and savoury flavour combined with a creamy texture. It is utterly delicious on toasted bread, draped over cooked scallops and other seafood. Lardo works really well with whelks, as it complements the earthy, oily texture of the shellfish. However, my secret pleasure is to just add it to fried eggs.

For this recipe, the sea snail represents the psychological, spiritual and physical sense of confinement that I experienced before sobriety. I had no self-control over the will to drink and I was preoccupied with self-indulgence. My healing journey only began once I accepted this sense of powerlessness. Acceptance was key. It enabled me to come out of my shell and explore a new found freedom.

The following dish is dedicated to Danny Craughwell (RIP), an excellent chef who reared Berkshire pigs and left us too soon.

Serves 4

Sea Snails 4
Lardo 4g
Mussel Stock 50ml
Dill Oil 5ml (see page 144)
Beach Herbs (as required)
Sea Salt 1g

1. Thoroughly wash sea snails in several changes of cold water (at least three times until the water runs clean).

2. Cover them in cold water and soak for 2 hours.

3. To cook: transfer the sea snails into a pot of boiling salted water and cook for 15 minutes.

4. Cool down and remove from the shells with a stick (or fork) and remove the worm like part and wash in cold water. Cut into small slivers.

5. In a pan add some of the mussel stock to sea snails and reheat.

6. Check for seasoning.

7. Add dill oil.

To Serve: Firstly, present the whelks in the shell and then proceed with the main dish, which is a bowl of whelks. To garnish use finely diced Lardo and sea herbs, such as sandwort, sea radish, purslane and pepper dulse.

Lardo

A huge thank you to my friend Cormac Handy who supplied the back fat for this dish, a chef and pig farmer, whose passion for all things local continues to inspire me.

Pork Back Fat 1000 g
Sea salt 25g
Sugar 75g
Black Peppercorns (crushed) 15g
Juniper berries 20g (crushed)
Garlic 8 cloves (crushed)
Thyme 4 sprigs
Bay Leaf 4g

1. Mix all the ingredients together.

2. Massage this mixture into the pork fat.

3. Vacuum pack and seal.

4. Transfer to the refrigerator with a weight on top.

5. Cure for 12 days, turning the fat every two days.

6. After the 12 days, rinse off all the cure mixture, pat dry.

7. Wrap in muslin cloth, secure with string and hang in the refrigerator or cold room for another two weeks.

Note: if you don't have access to a vacuum pack, use a zip lock bag, making sure that you remove all the air before closing the bag.

Beef with Horseradish and Waffles

This dish is about peace and harmony and is dedicated to all who tirelessly worked at the Anglo/Irish Secretariat Maryfield in Belfast, where I had the privilege of being head chef from 1996 to 1997. I cooked for the key players involved in negotiating what was to become The Belfast or Good Friday Agreement of 1998. Work meetings were often held over dinner, and I like to think that food played a role, albeit a small one, in supporting peace in Northern Ireland.

Serves 4

Castlemine Beef Fillet (Dry Aged) 200g
Pickled Black Garlic 5g
Pickled Elderberries 2g
Sea Salt – a pinch
Cured Egg Yolk 1

Horseradish Emulsion

Horseradish 200g
Sunflower Oil 300ml
Scurvygrass 2g
Egg Yolks 2

Cured Egg Yolk

Egg Yolk 1
Salt 200g
Dried Horseradish Skin Powder 2g

Waffle

Butter 50g
Beef Fat 100g
Eggs 4
Sugar 100g
Milk 600ml
Flour 700g
Baking Powder 2g

1. Place the horseradish, scurvygrass and sunflower oil into a vacuum bag and seal. Sous vide (cook in a water bath) at 62°C for 8 hours. Alternatively, place the ingredients into a pan and cover with tin foil and place in an oven at the same temperature – for the same time.

2. To cure the egg yolk: in a small bowl gently place in the egg yolk and add half of the horseradish salt. Cover completely with the remaining salt. Leave in the refrigerator for 24 hours. Remove the egg yolk and rinse in cold water. Dehydrate at 55°C for 12 to 15 hours. Alternatively, place on a tray in an oven at the same time and temperature.

3. Make batter for waffles by mixing all the ingredients together. Allow to rest.

4. Finely dice the beef (but not too fine) and add elderberries and black garlic. Check for seasoning.

5. Strain the horseradish oil and proceed to make an emulsion (like a mayonnaise) with the egg yolks.

6. Cook the waffles.

To Serve: Place the beef into a bowl with the horseradish emulsion on top and finish with grated cured egg yolk. Serve the waffles on the side.

Note: Scurvygrass can be found in saltmarshes and seashores and has a similar flavour to wasabi.

Salad of Organic Vegetables

This is one of those salads that consists of a wide variety of ingredients, primarily sourced from Joe and Margaret Bohan's organic farm in Galway.

Each ingredient has a role to play in bringing the whole dish together. The contrasting textures are complemented by sweet, sour, salty and bitter. Symbolically, this dish represents inner beauty and epitomises pureness, something that in the early days of my drinking I could never have found appealing, as I would have preferred more complex, rich dishes.

As a sober alcoholic, one of the things I enjoy most is simplicity, and in particular the elegance of these ingredients in their natural state. This dish is a reminder of how far I have come, and how much healing I have been blessed with.

The way all the ingredients work together to make a whole dissolves the illusion that happiness can be achieved in isolation. It is, therefore, a homage to interconnectedness, togetherness and companionship. It is a call to rejoice in the reality that we all need each other.

Serves 4

Baby Fennel 1
Red Chicory 1
Tomatoes 200g
Frizzy – a few plouches
Peas 50g
Radish 4
Heirloom Carrots 2
Turnip Small 4
Dandelion Leaves 4
Toasted Sesame Seeds 5g

Dressing:
Sesame Oil 2 tablespoons
White Miso 50g
Tamari 1 tablespoon
Ginger – a small piece 5g (grated)
Rice Wine Vinegar
2 tablespoons

1. Cut the baby fennel into 4 pieces and char on a hot grill.
2. Blanch the carrots in boiling salted water and refresh in iced water.
3. Thinly slice the radishes, cut tomatoes in half.
4. To make the dressing, blend all the ingredients together (if it's too thick thin out with a little water).
5. Place the dressing into a bowl and add the vegetables. Toss in the dressing.

To Serve: Arrange neatly on a plate (or bowl) and sprinkle with toasted sesame seeds.

Fermented Apples, Timut Pepper and Aromatic Flowers

This dish epitomises my life. It represents the old and new and the long slow process of coming out of the darkness of addiction into the light of sobriety – just like the apples in the chamber being transformed into something totally new.

Eating *fermented apple* is a time to pause and feel our connection to the very source of all that we are, and all that we may still become.

It is my dish of hope.

Serves 4

Apples 4
Flowers to Garnish
Sea Salt a pinch
Timut Pepper to season

1. Peel apples, vacuum pack and transfer to a fermentation chamber set to 60°C for 8 weeks. Alternatively, you can use a rice cooker (or slow cooker) at the 'keep warm' setting. Whatever cooker you use, make sure that it doesn't have an auto-off feature.

2. The apples will be very fragile. Carefully remove from the bag (keeping any residual liquid).

3. Purée 2 of the apples in a blender and pass through a sieve. Season with salt and timut pepper. Roughly chop the remaining 2 apples.

4. Spread some of the apple purée evenly 2cm in thickness on a mat or non-stick parchment and dry in an oven at 55°C overnight until it has a leather-like texture.

5. Cut into triangles.

6. Add the chopped apple to the remaining apple purée.

To Serve: Transfer the chopped apple mixture on a plate. Arrange the dried apple triangles on top and garnish with flowers.

Note: The Irish Peach apple is ideal for this dish. However, Granny Smith or Pink Ladies will work just as well.

REKINDLING THE FIRE

Chapter IV
Continental Menu
Acceptance

I reflect on being a sober alcoholic every day. It is something I am exceptionally grateful for, as I am aware thoroughly of how lucky I am to have survived.

It is not easy though. I bring the alcoholic with me everywhere I go. Moods, like the seasons, fluctuate and change. Some days are easier than others. Some dark, others not so much. My body and mind constantly remind me that I have to continually make a choice to abstain from my desires and compulsions. Over the years this has become easier, although it was not always like this. In the early days of sobriety I was plagued with bouts of seething resentment, rage and self-hate. I was, however, incredibly fortunate to find the support that I needed at a time in my life when I was about to give up.

The time-worn statement that 'you have to reach rock bottom before you are ready to give up', is true. I certainly reached the point where I was prepared to die. I could no longer go on with the life that had ravaged so much of my body and emotions, and yet making any change at all seemed so far out of reach that it felt impossible. I was in limbo, stuck on a cliff edge overlooking an abyss that I knew I had to journey across if I was to hold on to the last thread of sanity. With no compass to navigate the terrain, and very little strength to draw upon, I took just one step forward. That first step was without doubt the hardest, and while others have been equally gruelling, the initial reach for help was the most challenging experience of my life. This was because I had to both stand up and be accountable. I had to reveal myself with all my tattered explanations and lies. I had to be real and vulnerable, without self-pity and excuses. I had to be honest. And yet, while this experience was laced with trauma, it was the beginning of a whole new chapter of my life, where I have achieved a life that I could never have dreamt. I now travel the world with my work, I teach others the art of cuisine, and I am once again a father, husband and brother. I can honestly say that I have everything in my life that I have ever wanted.

This chapter is a homage to honesty. Honesty is not about being noble, righteous or full of ethical values. It is about being truthful. In relation to food, honesty is about connecting into the true essence and quality of your ingredients. It is about an unprocessed state of naturalness that holds a secret ingredient from which life itself springs forth.

In addition to honesty, these dishes celebrate my love of seasonal cuisine, my adventures on the continent and my journey into sobriety.

We live in a society that tends to make us feel uncomfortable with pain and suffering. We push these experiences away, try to change them and even live in denial. A symptom of this is that we run toward experiences that alleviate our suffering: alcohol, extravagant lifestyles and rich, opulent food choices. When we strip away the chaos and remove all these lavish trimmings, we are left with an essence and innate beauty that is quite simply remarkable.

The first dish is in honour of the humble tomato. It's about the quality of the tomato and seasonality.

Cooking in season is about utilising available, locally-sourced food, as well as food provenance. Eating seasonal produce has health benefits also: tomatoes, for instance, are cooling to the body, and therefore should be consumed in the summer months.

I once bought some tomatoes in a market in Barcelona; I went home and served them in the burning midday sun, with just a touch of salt and olive oil. I can still taste summer when I think of tomatoes. As I enjoyed the visual feast before me, I found the simplicity of the meal strangely comforting, even calming. I eventually cut into the juicy, sweet, mouth-watering ripe flesh and, all at once, the subtle notes of pine mixed with gentle peppery sweetness opened up a whole new world of taste for me.

That afternoon in Barcelona I realised that how an ingredient is handled and prepared before consumption (whether it is vegetable, animal or fish), has a profound effect upon the flavour and character of the dish. In other words, the quality of the *intention* behind both the harvesting and the cooking processes profoundly affect our food experience. Food, cooked in hectic kitchens with angry chefs and demanding guests, can of course produce excellent cuisine, but here in Barcelona, I prepared my lunch slowly with love and care, and importantly, I left the tomato in its natural, unaltered state of poised beauty. In many ways this simple meal was one of my most treasured life-moments.

The celeriac and chard plate is a take on a roasted whole celeriac, which we had during a college tour to La Rochelle, France. The fish head and tails is dedicated to David Bowie, whose music took me away from the grey Galway of the early 1970s. Both these dishes pay respect to utilising every part of an ingredient, thereby reducing waste. This is an analogy for acceptance: that every aspect of life has value, even our most challenging encounters. When we value every part of an ingredient we are engaging in a holistic exercise of honouring the life-force that the food offers, as well as acknowledging symbolically that every aspect of nature (including humans) are part of a natural ecosystem: that we are all connected.

The risotto is really about a summer that I spent in Italy, mostly in and around Piedmont and Tuscany. This dish celebrates the rice plantations in the Po Valley, and a wonderful bowl of roasted beets that I enjoyed in Lucca.

Finally, the plum cake is about the people of Bosnia, and Sarajevo in particular, where the most distinctive plants of this region are plums (Sljiva). During the plum season (August), they can be seen everywhere: on the side of the road, in markets and in Sarajevo's parks.

When I think of plums, I think of Bosnia.[3]

---

3 I served in Bosnia with SFOR and had the privilege of running a kitchen in Butmir from 1998 to 1999, where all the staff were local Bosniaks, Croats and Serbs.

Continental Menu

Acceptance

Tomato

Roast Celeriac with Parsnip and Chard

Fish Heads and Tails

Beetroot Risotto

Plum Cake

This menu invites you to sit in your 'true' essence, to connect mindfully with all that you are – that which is whole – right now – even when life appears otherwise.

Tomato

Serves 4

Beef Tomatoes 1kg
Heirloom Tomatoes 12
Cherry Tomatoes 12
(Yellow, Green)
Basil 1 Bunch
Thyme – a few sprigs
Rapeseed Oil – a dash
Borage Flowers 4
Achill Island Sea Salt 10g

You will need muslin cloth.
If you don't have muslin,
a chemical-free, clean
tea-towel will work, or a
coffee filter.

1. Roughly chop the beef tomatoes. Add salt and basil. Mix well.

2. Place the tomatoes into a muslin cloth and tie up, leaving enough string.

3. Tie the tomatoes wrapped in muslin to the shelf in your refrigerator and place a clean bowl underneath.

4. Leave overnight to drip through clean muslin cloth. Do not force through.

5. You now have a wonderful tomato essence or consommé.

6. Cover and place in the refrigerator.

7. Cut some cherry tomatoes in half. Lightly salt and dehydrate in a low oven 60°C, until almost dry.

8. Lightly score the remaining tomatoes. Blanch in boiling water and refresh in iced water.

9. Remove skins. Marinate the tomatoes in rapeseed oil and thyme.

10. Dehydrate the tomato skins until crisp.

To Serve: Place marinated tomatoes into a bowl, add tomato skins, semi dried tomatoes and borage flowers. Pour tomato essence onto the plate.

Note: You can pass the leftover tomato pulp through a sieve and spread it out onto a silomat and dehydrate. When it's dry, put it through a spice blender to make a tomato powder, which will bring another dimension to the dish.

Roast Celeriac with Parsnip and Chard

Serves 2

Medium-size Celeriac 1
Parsnips 200g (washed and peeled)
Cream 75ml
Butter 100g
Thyme – a few sprigs
Rainbow Chard 200g
Celeriac Oil 50ml
Milk 50ml
Salt and Pepper

1. Dehydrate the leaves and make a powder.

2. Roast the celeriac in seaweed and salt dough (see page 143) for 1 hour.

3. Remove celeriac from the pastry shell, peel the skin away and trim then cut into portions by using a round pastry 6 x 4 cm cutter.

4. Roughly chop the parsnip. Transfer to a pan, add milk and simmer until done. Drain and retain the cooking liquor.

5. Place the celeriac trim and the cooked parsnips into a blender and blitz, slowly adding the cooking liquor from the parsnips. Pass through a fine sieve.

6. Check for seasoning and finish with a good dollop of butter.

7. Transfer the purée to a Siphon/cream whip and charge with 2 chargers. Keep warm.

8. Caramelise the celeriac rounds in foaming butter and thyme, keep warm.

9. Wilt the chard in a little butter.

To Serve: Place the celeriac round onto a warmed plate, then the celeriac and parsnip mix on top and garnish with wilted chard. Dust with the celeriac leaf powder and drizzle with celeriac oil and serve.

Note: Do not discard the stalks of the chard. Weigh them, add 2% salt and either vacuum pack, or place into a Kilner jar with a weight on and leave to ferment for 5–7 days. Once opened, transfer to a refrigerator and it will last for about 3 months. The skin from the celeriac and parsnip peelings can also be dehydrated and powdered in a spice grinder.

Fish Heads and Tails

"There's a sailor who eats only fish heads and tails" (David Bowie, Amsterdam).

The head, throat, cheek and the tail are utilised in this recipe. This particular dish is derived from the humble pollack. The cheeks are succulent and sweet, which complements the intense gelatinous nature of the throat, called kokotxas by the Basques, and held in high esteem. On a recent trip to San Sebastian, I had the most amazing food at the restaurant aptly named Kokotxa. The tail was brushed with garum and grilled until charred.

If you are not confident about filleting the fish, ask your local fishmonger to do it for you.

Serves 4

Pollack Throats 4
Pollack Cheeks 4
Pollack Tails 4
Garum 5g (see page 81)
Butter 10g
Pil Pil Sauce 20ml
Achill Island Sea Salt 5g

1. Make the Pil Pil (see below).
2. Lightly cure the fish with sea salt leave for 20 minutes.
3. Rinse the fish in cold water, dry and put aside.
4. Melt the butter and add the garum.
5. Brush the fish with garum and butter mix and grill. Continue to baste with the garum and butter until done.

To Serve: Arrange the tail, cheek and throats onto a plate and sauce, serve with a simple salad or buttered potatoes.

Note: The tail will take a little longer to cook.

Pil Pil Sauce

Traditionally this sauce is made by cooking bacalao (salt cod) skin on in a garlic/chilli scented olive oil. Once the fish is cooked, the oil and the white fish protein are separated and whisked together to form the sauce. Another way is to cook the fish trim and the bones in the olive oil instead of the fillets.

Salted Cod 1 fillet (skin on)
Olive Oil 250 ml
Garlic Cloves (thinly sliced)
Chilli ½ of a Small One

1. Place the olive oil in a pan. Add the sliced garlic and chilli and gently cook.

2. With a slotted spoon, remove the chilli and garlic.

3. Cook the cod at a low temperature.

4. When the cod fillets are cooked, remove from the pan.

5. What remains is the milky white protein and the olive oil.

6. Decant the oil into a jug and place the white protein into a suitable pan (or bowl).

7. Whisk the white protein and add the olive oil slowly until you achieve a mayonnaise type consistency.

8. Keep warm and serve.

Garum

Mackerel, Herring, Smelt (Whole) 1kg
Salt 160g (16%)
Water 450ml
Kilner Jar 1 (sterilised)

1. Remove the gills only.

2. Blend the chopped fish guts, bones and eyes with the salt and the water until a smooth paste is achieved.

3. Place the mixture into a glass jar and scrape down the inside of the jar. Cover the surface of the garum with cling film.

4. Cover the container with a lid and ferment in a dark place at room temperature for 3 months stirring every day. The ancient Romans and Carthaginians used just fish and salt (usually 18% salt placed into a suitable container and fermented for 9 to 12 months). The high percentage of salt prevents spoilage. Important to stir regularly. If you see any mould, just remove it. The results are amazing.

Beetroot Risotto

Serves 4

Arborio Rice 200g
Beetroot 1kg
Beetroot Stock/Juice 1 litre
Butter 70g
Shallots 100g (finely diced)
Smoked Gubbeen Cheese 60g
Salt and Pepper

1. Bake one whole beetroot and dice, then juice the remaining beetroot.

2. Add some of the butter to a suitable pan and sweat the diced shallot until slightly translucent.

3. Add the rice and stir until each grain of rice has been coated in the butter.

4. Add a ladle full of hot beetroot juice into the rice until the rice has absorbed the beetroot juice.

5. Repeat this procedure until the rice has swollen and is almost tender.

6. The rice should be soft but not chalky. It is usually cooked in 20 minutes.

7. Remove from the heat and add the diced beetroot, butter and half of the grated gubbeen.

8. Check for seasoning, cover and allow to rest for 3–4 minutes.

To Serve: Eat immediately with some grated gubbeen on the side.

Note: The beetroot pulp left from the juicing process can be dehydrated at 55°C, or in an oven overnight. When it is completely dry, transfer to a spice grinder and blitz. The result is an amazing beetroot powder. Store in an airtight container.

Plum Cake

This is a take on the traditional French clafoutis, which is a dessert usually made with cherries. You can also use raspberries, gooseberries or rhubarb. In this recipe I am using plums and slivovitz (plum brandy, a traditional drink in many Eastern European countries).

Serves 4

Plums 400g
Slivovitz 20ml (Plum Brandy)
Brown Sugar 10g
Flour 40g
Eggs 2
Sugar (Caster) 35 g
Milk 175g
Icing Sugar for Dusting

1. In a bowl, beat the eggs and sugar together until the sugar is well dissolved.

2. Add the milk and sieved flour. Mix well and strain.

3. In a sur le plat (or oven proof dish) add some butter and heat. Add halved plums and brown sugar and cook in the oven for 5 minutes.

4. Remove plums from the oven and add the slivovitz and flambé. Once the alcohol has burned off, pour the batter into the dish.

5. Bake at 180°C for 30 minutes or until golden brown and set.

To Serve: Dust with icing sugar and serve with whipped cream. It is best to serve immediately, as it will collapse and deflate. If it does collapse not to worry as it still tastes wonderful.

Note: Sometimes, I substitute the plums with salted ones (Umeboshi), which brings sweet and sour notes to the clafoutis. The clafoutis can also be made in tartlet moulds, cast iron pans and baking dishes.

Chapter V
South East Asian Inspired Menu
Self-Reflection

In 2004 my son, Jason, and I went backpacking to South East Asia. It was an opportunity to get to know him better and rekindle our bond. We journeyed from Bangkok to Cambodia: dirt tracks, palm trees, sugar cane, the iconic Ankor Wat, Tonle Sap, the 'killing fields' in Phnom Penh and on to Vietnam; from Ho Chi Minh City (Saigon) to Hanoi. Laos, Malaysia, Singapore and on to Hong Kong. We travelled overland by train or bus.

Out of all the places visited, it was the ancient town of Hội An (now a dedicated UNESCO World Heritage site) that affected me the most profoundly, and in turn changed my life-course. Situated on the coast of central Vietnam, the town of Hội An, with it's beautiful pagodas and endless walls of golden shower trees is nestled near the mouth of the Thu Bon River in the Quang Nam Province.

The town is famous for its thriving South-East Asian trading port that dates back to the 15th century. Its success was due to having easy access to the Thu Bon River and its vast, intricate waterways. To this day the river remains the heart and soul of Hội An's prismatic traditional townscape, of which the old town is the setting for world famous full moon festivals of light. During these old festivals of music, poetry and dance, people flock to the shores of the Thu Bon River to release candle-lit sacred lanterns onto the water in the dark of the night.

It is a festival laden with the symbolism of Vietnam's national flower, the lotus. Every part of this striking flower is used extensively in Vietnamese cooking, including its petals, stems, pods and root. Known as the 'flower of dawn', the journey that the lotus undertakes to blossom is remarkable. Having its roots immersed in muddy water, every night at sunset the flower retreats into its murky pond. At dawn it pushes its way through the darkness toward the light to flower once again. Universally this is a flower with a penetrating allegory, and during our visit to Hội An I was blessed that this blossom became a life-long metaphor for my own journey toward the light: one that subsequently became a daily ritual of commitment and release, of letting go and beginning every day anew.

During my stay at Hội An an unexpected encounter with the power of mindfulness unfolded. I had become fascinated by the family-run rice plantations that fanned in all directions from the outskirts of the city. One afternoon I spent some time watching a group of farmers tending their land. This was a seasoned way of life, where each grain of rice produced would hold the essence of previous generations who had gathered for centuries with the sole purpose of producing food that resonates with the heart of authenticity. I was taken by the sense of peace that emanated from their methodical, yet graceful movement. Nothing was forced or laboured. There was a sense that each movement flowed into the next, and that the art of farming was not separate from the crop being brought to life. The farmer and the land required each other: it was a continuous melody of energetic exchange, a deeply connected form of communication that had no spoken word. I had not witnessed anything like this before. It was as if the people, and this place, were intrinsically connected; the farmer and their land were one patterned ecosystem.

I was struck by the idea that food produced with such love was imbued with the energy of the caretaker, and as I witnessed this scene before me, I vowed to explore this elegant grace in my cooking. It was here in the fields near Hội An that I committed to a philosophy that became the foundation of my life's work – a way of cooking and living that inspired my every waking moment: to 'let food speak for itself'.

Such musing on that soft afternoon captivated my poise, so much so that I sat for some time lost in thoughtless reverie. Seconds, minutes, maybe even hours passed. This was the first time that I had dared to be fully present. My body felt both heavy and light at the same time. It was as if I would never move again, yet at the same time, like a bamboo leaf my energy lightly danced in a breeze of timeless wonder.

My breath deepened naturally in response to the scent of crisp green foliage intermingled with mists of coconut rain hitting against well-worn dirt tracks. My senses were calm, yet alive. I could feel the vital energy of the land running through the veins of the earth and, just as the sun penetrated my awakening, I sensed a gentle evening wind gathering on distant hills. I arose to an innocent backdrop of children singing. Somehow I knew their songs were about home, and I felt an overwhelming desire to find my son and prepare for the evening festival.

During the full moon festival residents from the old quarter switch off all their electric lights. Candles and bright silk lanterns light up the traditional narrow streets. The riverside timber frame houses, with their ancient hand-carved motifs, are transformed into a brilliant backdrop of colour and magical displays. Luminous lime green, blood red rose, radiant turmeric orange dancing in mustard yellow light, is reflected onto the dark velvet tones of the river and her banks. This enchanted setting transforms into an awe-inspiring ceremony, where small lotus lanterns are set adrift on the river in memory of the ancestors. Traditionally, people from all over the region would come to pray for love, wisdom, healing, and grace.

It was truly captivating.

This magical scene was made all the more alluring by distant scents of roasted coffee blended with toasted pepper spice, aromatic herbs and fragrant honeysuckle blossoms.

This timeless sense-filled experience was where I released a prayer lantern from a small sky-blue wooden boat.

I didn't know it at the time, but this poignant moment on the riverbank marked the beginning of a completely new period of my life.

It was here that I began a reflective journey looking back at my life, and in particular how addiction and alcoholism had impacted my family. At the time I had been sober for about two and a half years, but I had not fully faced my 'demons'. Beginning the process of introspection during my visit to Hội An was really difficult, as it brought up so much guilt and remorse. But, after watching the lantern sailing off into the darkness, I sensed the wind of change gathering momentum.

I knew I had to have a hard look at myself and what I had become.

This didn't happen overnight, rather it was (and is) a continual process of self-reflection. For me, reality can be very challenging and difficult to bear. Yet, facing the darkness and digging deep to find some form of self-acceptance has been the catalyst that has helped me to change.

How did I do this? Through cooking.

What I have learnt from the farmers of Hội An is that being in rhythm with a daily practice, such as cooking, releases me from my tendency for self-destructive behaviour because it quietens my emotions and creates space for other more creative, healing pursuits to unfold.

Over the years I have discovered a practice of mindful recovery. Every time I cook I move into a place of quiet contemplation and begin a journey of freedom from the bondage of self. I release the ego and allow the ingredients of the dish to 'speak to me'. From here, I am able to become part of a process that connects me to something so beautiful that I cannot help but fall into a deep sense of awe. It is in this state that I have no regrets.

The following menu is about gratitude, which counteracts negativity and all the other illusions from my past that resulted in me losing a sense of what really matters in life: my family.

South East Asian Inspired Menu

Self-Reflection

Bao

Goi Cuon Spring Roll Pork-Belly

Lobster Infused Royale with Thai Curry

Vegetable Amok

Vietnamese Coffee Dessert

This menu invites you to experience cooking as a process of letting go of the past and beginning every day anew.

Each time you cook these dishes, approach them as if you have never tried them before.

Enjoy each taste as if it is the first and the last time.

Be Present.

Bao

Also known as steamed buns, Bao can be a meal in itself. They can be filled with pork, lamb, fish or vegetables. Although it can be a long and complicated process, once you master the basic technique it becomes second nature. These warm, white cushions of deliciousness are totally addictive and well worth the effort. Long after my first experience of eating Bao in Hong Kong, I was staging with the Maestro Claude Bosi in his Hibiscus restaurant in 2014, when the head chef, Ian Scaramuzza, suggested that I try Bao on Lexington Street in Soho. Bao is a small Taiwanese street-food inspired restaurant. Although you may have to queue, it is definitely worth it. I frequently travel to London whether it is work related or visiting family and a visit to Bao is always on the agenda.

Yield: 20

Instant Yeast 10g
Water 215g (tepid)
Rice Wine vinegar 6g
Vegetable Oil 20g
Hong Kong Flour 400g
Potato Starch 135g
Salt 2g
Baking Powder 12g
Cold Water 12g

1. Dissolve the yeast into the warm water. Add vinegar, oil and salt.
2. Mix all the dry ingredients and sieve.
3. Add the dry ingredients to the wet ones and knead with a dough hook for 10 minutes.
4. Transfer the dough to a lightly oiled bowl. Cover with a clean cloth and proof for 45 minutes (or until it has doubled in size).
5. Transfer the dough into a mixing machine.
6. Dilute the baking powder into the cold water and add to the dough. Mix on a low speed for 10 minutes.
7. Place the dough onto a suitable surface. Keep covered.
8. Scale the dough into 35g pieces and roll into an oval shape.
9. Spray baos with butter spray and place a square of greaseproof paper in the centre then fold over. Remove the greaseproof paper.
10. Cut squares of parchment or greaseproof paper and place a bao on each cover with a clean cloth and allow to prove until doubled in size. It usually takes 60 to 90 minutes.
11. Steam for 8 to 10 minutes.

To Serve: Slow roasted neck, shoulder of pulled pork or lamb is the ideal filling. However, this one is using kimchi. It can be garnished with pickled julienne of mooli, carrot or spring onion, coriander and kimchi.

Note: Hong Kong flour is an all-purpose flour that is highly bleached. It is available at most specialist shops. When you add the baking powder, you let it rest for 10 minutes before rolling. Because it's double leavened it can deteriorate quickly so you need to work fast. Slow roasted neck or shoulder of pulled pork or lamb is the ideal filling and can be garnished with pickled julienne of mooli, carrot or spring onion, coriander and kimchi.

Vegetable Amok

Amok is a traditional Cambodian stew of chicken or shellfish. It is usually cooked in a banana leaf bowl on top of the stove. However, this version is plant based.

Serves 4

Diced Tofu (firm) 200g
Soy Sauce 2 tablespoons
Lime Juice 2 tablespoons
Diced Sweet Potato 300g
Carrot Medium 1 (Sliced on the Angle)
Peas 10g
Large Shiitake Mushroom 5
Garlic Cloves – Crushed 4
Diced Red Pepper 1
Kaffir Lime Leaves 6 to 8
Red Miso 2 tablespoons
Palm Sugar 2g
Chillies 3
Turmeric ½ teaspoon
Coconut Milk 1–2 cans
Vegetable Stock 200ml

1. Add tofu and lime juice to a wok or large pan, and cook for 2 minutes or until the liquid has evaporated. Continue cooking until the tofu is golden brown. Transfer to another pan.

2. Add the sweet potatoes, carrots, mushrooms and peppers.

3. Add the remaining ingredients and cook on top of the stove, or cover with a lid and cook in the oven for 35–45 minutes.

To serve: Line a bowl with banana leaves and add the amok.

Lobster Infused Royale with Coconut and Lemongrass

Serves 4

Lobster Oil 1 teaspoon
(see page 145)
Eggs 4
Milk 150ml
Cream 150ml
Cooked Lobster Claw
(diced) 20g

Coconut and Lemongrass Espuma

Coconut Milk 250ml
Lemongrass 2 sticks
Xanthan Gum 1g
Curry Powder
1 tablespoon
Sea Salt to season
Sugar to season

1. Prepare the eggs by removing the tops. Sterilise in boiling water and remove the membrane. Turn upside down and leave in an egg carton until required.

2. Gently heat the coconut milk and add crushed lemon grass. Leave to infuse for 2 hours.

3. For the lobster custard: heat milk and cream together. Add lobster oil and 2 eggs. Blend until smooth.

4. Strain the custard into a jug (let it stand for a few minutes and skim off any foam).

5. Two-thirds fill the prepared egg shells with the custard and place into a water bath/bain marie and gently cook until custard is set. Alternatively, transfer eggs into an egg carton (stability). Add a tea towel and enough water to the tray then add the eggs. Cover with tin foil and bake in the oven 150°C until the custard is set (35–40 minutes approx).

6. Strain the lemongrass infused coconut milk and blend in the xanthan gum with a hand held blender, season with sugar and salt.

7. Place into a siphon with 2 charges.

To Serve: Add some diced lobster to the egg. Pipe in the coconut and lemongrass foam. Smooth over with a pallet knife. Dust with curry powder and serve in an egg cup, or a small egg carton lined with straw.

Goi Cuon: Spring Roll with Pork Belly

Serves 4

Pork Belly 100g

Baby Gem Lettuce Leaves 4

Mint – a few leaves

Chives 1 tablespoon

Rice Paper 1 pack

Mooli 10g (julienne)

Carrot 10g (julienne)

Dipping Sauce

Sunflower Oil
2 tablespoons

Sesame Oil – a dash

Garlic Cloves 2 (crushed to a paste)

Hoisin sauce
6 tablespoons

Peanut Butter
2–3 tablespoons

Water – a splash

Red Chilli 1 (finely diced)

1. Slow roast the pork belly for 3 hours at 140°C.

2. To construct the roll: soak the rice paper in cold water for a few seconds until it is soft and pliable.

3. Lay out the rice paper and add your prepared ingredients and the sliced pork. Don't be tempted to add too many ingredients because it would be harder to roll.

4. For the dipping sauce add all the ingredients except the water. Check for consistency, then add water to achieve the desired consistency. It should be thick enough so that it adheres to the Goi Cuon.

To Serve: Place spring rolls onto a plate and serve the dipping sauce on the side.

Note: The traditional Goi Cuon includes pork and shrimp. However, you can construct your own versions with different ingredients.

Vietnamese Coffee

This is a take on the much loved traditional Vietnamese coffee.

Serves 4

Sweetened Condensed
Milk 1 can
Espressos 4
Leaves of Gelatine 2
Sugar 4g
Egg Yolks 4

1. Soak the gelatine in cold water.

2. Make four espressos then add one leaf of gelatine and mix well. Strain and pour into coffee cups, cool and refrigerate until set.

3. Put egg yolks, sugar and condensed milk into a bowl and whisk over a pan of hot water (bain marie) for 5 minutes until ribbon stage then add gelatine. Do not allow the bowl to come in contact with the hot water.

4. Chill in a refrigerator and transfer to a piping bag.

To Serve: Pipe the egg yolk/condensed milk sabayon over the set coffee and serve.

Chapter VI

Nordic Menu

Transience

Being sober allows me to do things beyond my wildest dreams, such as travel, teach and work with internationally acclaimed chefs in Michelin-starred restaurants all over the world. This is in stark contrast to where I used to be when drinking. Before sobriety I lived a life permanently plagued with paranoia, fear, shame, anger and disgust, with regular bouts of homelessness, sleeping in ditches and derelict houses. I often remind myself of these experiences to fully appreciate my life now. It is short of a miracle that I no longer 'come to' in strange places and situations, such as police cells (experiences that often resulted in court appearances) with no recollection of how I got there, or what I had done. Blackouts are a terrifying phenomenon. For example, I could be drinking with a group of friends (not drunk) and behaving and appearing 'normal', and then I come to in a different town, with no memory of how I got there, or with whom I had been. I could go in and out of these episodes several times a day, and sometimes they could last for days at a time. My physical and mental health was a mess. I was a nervous wreck, but I paid no attention to this. When the cravings raged I returned without hesitation to the endless, dark cycle of self-destruction.

The menu for this chapter is a metaphor for change. It is an offering of hope to all those who still live in this kind of darkness. It is my desire that this chapter, and the whole book for that matter, can provide a glimmer of light into the shadows. That I have been able to completely turn my life around is testament that others can as well.

There is an enormous latent potential hidden within everyone cursed with the illness of addiction. It just takes time, patience and a lot of self-forgiveness to find it.

This chapter is also inspired by my experience of staging, travelling, talking and, more importantly, listening to the people of Norway, Finland, Denmark, Sweden and Iceland.

Over the last decade the new Nordic model has been adopted throughout Europe and the US, representing a profound reaction to classical French cuisine. A lot of chefs have staged in Noma and brought their ethos back to their kitchens. I was very interested in this new phenomenon and had to see what it was all about. So in 2016 I accepted a position as a stagiaire at the ground-breaking three Michelin-starred restaurant Maaemo, in Oslo, with Chef Esben Holmboe Bang and his amazing team. It was a totally mind-blowing experience as I was exposed to new techniques, ingredients and ways of thinking about cooking, such as using ants to bring out acidity in a dish. It was an experience completely different from my classical training.

Esben (a Dane) has taken Norwegian traditional dishes, such as Rømmegrøt, or sour cream porridge to new levels. Indeed, the lamb heart dish on this menu is a take on a classic soubise dish using Nordic techniques.

I also had the privilege of staging with the legendary Finnish chef: Sasu Laukkonen, at his Helsinki restaurant ORA. Sasu is an amazing guy and a brilliant chef. His enthusiasm for his craft and local ingredients is infectious. I have had the privilege of dining in restaurants all over the world, including Frantzén in Stockholm and Geranium in Copenhagen, which was utterly amazing.

I am extremely fortunate to be where I am today; to still be involved in cookery and to be in a position to pass on a love of cooking to a younger generation. For example, recently, we hosted a dinner for the speakers at the *Food on the Edge Symposium* and the highly accomplished chefs: Sasu, Matt Orlando (Amass) and Douglas McMaster (Silo) worked alongside students in our kitchens at the *Galway International Hotel School at GMIT*. It is during moments like these that I feel compelled to share my story. Not out of ego or in search of approval, but quite simply to show others that they too can change and that a life such as mine is not out of reach.

When I look back on my life, one of the things I am most grateful for is the opportunity to experience Nordic cuisine. It has not only transformed my cooking, but given me the strength and resolve to continue along a path of sobriety. It is difficult to put into words exactly why Nordic cuisine speaks to me so much. There is so much about it that I love and would like to share. For now, I ponder upon a dish created by Esben Holmboe Bang: mackerel with elm shoots that taste of sweet nuts and marzipan, served with apple jelly and ramson oil. The refreshing vibrant green tones of this dish dance off the plate with an energy and serenity that propel me into a state of peacefulness. It is in these quiet moments of reflective contemplation that the spirit of Nordic cuisines speaks: it invites us to remove the clutter of life and the chaos of our own illusions and, in so doing, we discover our 'true essence', something that exists in us all. This is nature at its very best: perfection in imperfection, beauty in the everyday, and freedom in the constraints of the struggle.

Living in relationship with the rawness of our nature is not all roses and sunshine, it is also about the clouds, hail-storms and the dark freezing cold nights. Put simply, the Nordic food experience has taught me how to see the best in myself and others, it has offered me an opportunity to live a life of acceptance with all my grey shades and incomplete stories, and for that I am eternally grateful.

A Brief Background to Nordic Cuisine:

In 2003 a new Nordic movement associated with Claus Meyer, Rene Redzepi and their restaurant Noma, came into being. Noma is a three-Michelin star, multiple award winning restaurant in Copenhagen, Denmark. In 2010, 2011, 2012, 2014, and 2021 it was ranked as the *Best Restaurant in the World* by Restaurant Magazine, and 2nd in 2019. Together, with a group of chefs, Meyer and Redzepi created a collaborative platform that completely re-invented Nordic cuisine. This creative food revolution has subsequently developed into a larger green Nordic agenda: 'to live in harmony with nature and create sustainable societies' and is supported by the Nordic Council of Ministers.[4]

With seasonality and terroir to the fore, this new generation of chefs tell a story about home, region, place and belonging. Chef Patron at three Michelin-starred restaurant Maaemo, Esben Holmboe Bang, notes that food must reflect 'who we are and what we are', and 'what we do here is ours alone, it has meaning here and only here'.[5] For Bang, this is Norway. He is cautious to use the phrase 'new Nordic cuisine', and is keen to emphasise that while there are similarities between different North European countries, their landscapes and environments are also quite different.

That said, there are common threads that run through this new Nordic movement: an emphasis upon pure, simple, fresh regionally-sourced ingredients, rather than importing exotic products:

> One distinction that is important to me is that the Norwegian kitchen we are part of has a different logic than the classic kitchen I grew up with. There you find a well-established classic hierarchy in which tenderloin is better than sirloin, scallops are better than mahogany clams, and where potatoes and other vegetables are side dishes. When I make food, I never think like that. A carrot or a Jerusalem artichoke has as much value as a fine cut of meat. Or greater. A two hundred-year-old mahogany clam tells a different – and in many ways richer – story than turbot. It tastes different and is, for me, more exciting. A herb that is picked at Ekebergasen in Oslo at six-thirty in the morning is more exclusive than a truffle flown in from Italy.
> *Chef Esben Holmboe Bang.*[6]

Nordic cuisine is inspired by, and dependent upon, locality. What makes each place specific is a combination of unique features: climate, soil, water, seasonality and culture. Increasingly, issues about

---

4 As laid out in their *Manifesto of the New Nordic Cuisine*. See: https://www.norden.org/en/declaration/our-vision-2030

5 Esben Holmboe Bang. 2018: p.36 Maaemo. English edition. Published by Maaemo. www.maaemo.no.

6 Esben Holmboe Bang. 2018: p.36 Maaemo.

food production and sustainability have come to the fore. There is an acknowledgment that the life-cycle of an ingredient (or produce) is an important part of the chef's story. Magnus Nilsson, former head chef at two Michelin-starred restaurant Fäviken (which closed its doors in 2019), believes that a dish will never be better than its produce. For him, what distinguishes a 'good and fantastic' meal is the very quality of the ingredients, how they are harvested, stored and prepared.

Nilsson lives in one of the most remote hinterlands in Sweden: Järpen, between the mountain Åreskutan and the deep, cold lake Kallsjön. Much of the year this surreal landscape is covered in snow and ice and during winter, temperatures often plummet to between -25°C to -35°C, so very little grows:

> It's flat, its trees, it's water, and it's on the way to nowhere. It is, therefore, extreme. And, in extremity, you discover something new in food.
> *Bill Buford. Writer. The New Yorker. Chef's Table. Volume I: Episode 5.*

Nilsson's focus on indigenous ingredients is an opportunity to reconnect with nature because the landscape within which he lives dictates which ingredients he can use. What is in season is combined with an array of foraged herbs, such as fireweed, meadowsweet and cardoons (a member of the thistle family) and wildflowers (he has mastered multiple ways to serve lupins: fresh, dried and roasted). In addition to being one of the most celebrated chefs in the world, Nilsson is noted for reviving many of the region's age-old techniques for preservation; drying, salting, pickling, smoking, storing and curing. Pickled apples, marigold, turnips and carrots, barley vinegar and cabbage kimchi would regularly feature at Fäviken. One of his highly acclaimed recipes is his rendition of a traditional Icelandic dish: 'preserved wild birds eggs in burnt sheep dung ash'.

In order to be loyal to his place-based philosophy Nilsson spent years chronicling local cooking methods that were almost extinct. For him, the use of traditional cooking methods is not, however, about going back to the old ways.[7] It is more about re-interpreting what works in a specific region, as well as having respect for the ingredients that you work with.

There is a preoccupation in modern Western culture to look constantly for 'new' ways of doing things, and as a result innovation and invention have become synonymous with ideas about creativity. However, pioneers of the new Nordic cuisine invite us to (re)consider tried and tested cooking techniques (some of which have existed since the time of the Vikings), while at the same time re-interpreting them within the context of modernity and food science. The result is a fusion of the old (local tradition) with the new (evolving cultural practice). In this sense, the new unfolds out of the old. It is part of a living process, a continuous cycle of death and rebirth that is fundamentally connected with nature, her elements and a dynamic human-environment relationship.

This leads to another common feature of the new Nordic food experience: the importance of biodiversity, small-scale animal husbandry and sustainability. Many of the features that define Nordic cuisine are similar to other food movements, such as the Organic and Slow Food revolutions, which grew out of a response to intensive factory-farming techniques and fast-food-lifestyles from the 1940s.[8] The

---

7 An endeavour that grew into a larger study of classic and new Nordic cooking: Magnus Nilsson. The Nordic Cookbook. 2015. Phaidon Press.

8 While many of the practices cited as organic methods have their origins in traditional societies from all over the world, the modern term 'organic agriculture' broadly refers to food that is not genetically modified, is produced sustainably and without toxic chemicals.

Key thought-leaders that pioneered the movement against farming with chemicals since the early 1900s include: Franklin King, Sir Albert and Gabrielle Howard, Rudolf Steiner, Lady Eve Balfour, and Masanobu Fukuoka. The actual term organic, however, was coined by Walter James, Lord Northbourne (one of Steiner's followers), in his book: Look to the Land (1940).

In terms of associations, the world's first advocacy group specifically established to promote 'organic' farming was the Australian Organic Farming and Gardening Society (AOFGS), founded in Sydney in October 1944. However, it was the formation of the International Federation of Organic Agriculture Movements (IFOAM) at Versailles, France, in 1972 that was key to the organic movement becoming a global phenomenon with a clear agenda and manifesto. Initiated by France's

organic movement in particular has been a powerful force, one that has inspired the development of countless organisations and communities throughout the world to adopt a slower, greener and more self-sufficient way of life. Indeed, the term 'organic' is now more synonymous with a lifestyle, not just a way of farming and food production, and it is central to other environmental debates concerned with climate change and biodiversity. As such, the definition has broadened and become a 'house-hold' term in relation to conversations about health and well-being.

Nature et Progrès, and the then President, Roland Chevriot, the founding members of IFOAM were: Rodale Press of the USA; the Soil Association of the UK; the Soil Association of South Africa; and the Swedish Biodynamic Association. Source: John Paul, Journal of Social Policy and Research, No. 2. 2010: 93-102.

Fennel Pollen

REKINDLING THE FIRE

Nordic Menu

Transience

Puffed Barley, Kohlrabi and Horseradish

Beetroot, Pineapple Weed, Strawberry and Rhubarb with
Pickled Rose Petals

Squid, Oyster, Watercress, Dill and Chicken Skin

Smoked Lambs Heart, Onion and Elderflower Vinegar

Fennel Granita, Skyr and Wild Bilberries

This menu invites you to dream your wildest dreams.

Puffed Barley, Kohlrabi, Kombucha and Horseradish

Serves 4

Kohlrabi 1
Organic Barley 200g
Horseradish 5g
Miso 2g
Kombucha, a dash
Rapeseed Oil, a dash
Sauerkraut Brine
(as required)

1. Cook the barley in boiling salted water for 35 to 40 minutes.

2. Drain and refresh under a cold tap. Leave to drain and dehydrate 50g of the barley.

3. Transfer the rest of the barley to a Kilner jar and add the miso which has been diluted in the sauerkraut brine. Seal and store in a cool place for 2 days.

4. Using a mandolin, thinly slice the kohlrabi and cut into rounds, add a little Kombucha and vacuum pack to compress the kohlrabi.

5. Dehydrate the kohlrabi leaves. When dry, pass through a spice grinder, sieve and store in an airtight container.

To Serve: Place a tablespoon of the cooked barley and miso mixture onto a suitable bowl, add a little finely grated horseradish, add three rounds of kohlrabi drizzle with a little oil, dust with the leaf powder and sprinkle over some deep fried barley puffs.

Note: Weigh the trimming from the kohlrabi and add 2% salt to it, vacuum pack or place in a Kilner jar and ferment for 5 to 7 days.

Beetroot, Pineapple Weed, Strawberry and Rhubarb with Pickled Rose Petals

The earthiness of the beets and the sweetness of the strawberry come nicely together with the pineapple weed, which brings subtle chamomile notes. The rhubarb brings a contrasting tartness. The inspiration for this dish comes from Sasu Laukkonen (the Chef Patron at ORA Restaurant in Helsinki) where I had the privilege of staging with his amazing team.

Serves 4

Baby Beetroot 4
Candy Beetroot 1
Golden Beetroot 1
Pineapple Weed 100g
Rhubarb 50g
Pickled Rose Petals 8
Strawberry 10g

1. Season baby beets with a little sea salt and a little rapeseed oil, wrap in tinfoil and bake at 160°C until cooked (35 to 40 minutes approximately).

2. Once cooked, cool down and remove the skin.

3. Thinly slice both the candy beetroot and the golden beetroot.

4. Lightly pickle the candy one and place the golden ones in iced water.

5. Cut the rhubarb into thin strips (julienne).

6. Finely dice the strawberry and add pineapple weed heads.

To Serve: Place strawberry dice on the centre of the plate, add whole baby beet, rhubarb and golden and candy beets. Garnish with pickled edible rose petals.

Squid, Oyster, Watercress, Dill and Chicken Skin

Serves 2

Squid 1 medium
Kelly's Oysters 2
Oyster Juice from shell
Watercress 65g
Dill Oil (see page 144)
Chicken Skin 150g
Rapeseed Oil 350 ml
Sea Salt 2g
Sea Lettuce (as required)

1. Clean the squid and remove tentacles. Open up like a book. Dry and lightly cure with sea salt for 8 minutes. Rinse in cold water and dry.

2. Place one piece of squid on top of the other. Wrap in cling film and freeze.

3. In a pan, place seasoned chicken skin onto silicone paper and fold over to cover. Place a weight on top (e.g. a smaller pan) and place in a hot oven 180°C until crisp.

4. Place oyster and juice into a blender. Add blanched and refreshed watercress and dill oil and blend well, adding rapeseed oil slowly (similar to making mayonnaise) to form an emulsion.

5. Season to taste. Place in a piping bag and refrigerate.

6. Meanwhile, remove cling film from the squid and slice very thin on a slicing machine or a mandolin.

7. Cook squid in boiling salted water for 10 to 15 seconds. Drain.

To Serve: Pipe oyster and watercress emulsion onto a bowl or the cleaned oyster shell, place squid on top and garnish with chopped chicken skin and sea lettuce.

Smoked Lamb's Heart, Onion and Elderflower Vinegar

Serves 4

Soubise Mix
Milk 400ml
Onions 200g
Sour Cream 50g
Nigella Seeds 2g

Brown Butter
Butter 60g

Elderflower Vinegar
(see page 148)

1. Poach the onions in the milk until well cooked (35 minutes).

2. Strain the onions and blend to a smooth paste adding a little milk to achieve a thick béchamel type consistency.

3. Add the sour cream, check for seasoning and keep warm.

4. Make brown butter: heat the butter to a brown colour, be careful not to burn it. Add some elderflower vinegar and strain through muslin cloth or a fine strainer.

To Serve: Fill a suitable dish with the soubise. Add the finely grated Lamb's heart over the soubise and pour a good tablespoon of the brown butter and elderflower vinegar mix in the centre. Sprinkle some toasted nigella seeds.

Smoked Lamb's Hearts

Lamb Heart 1
Brine (see page 34)
Hay (as required)

1. Place the lamb heart into the brine and refrigerate for 24 hours.

2. Remove the heart from the brine and dry with kitchen paper.

3. Transfer a sufficient amount of hay to the bottom of a deep tray.

4. Light the hay and place a perforated tray over, add the lamb heart, cover with tin foil and then cling film to prevent any smoke escaping.

5. Smoke for 2 hours.

6. Dehydrate the heart at 55°C overnight or until completely dry. Alternatively, you can place it in an oven at the same temperature.

Fennel Granita, Skyr and Wild Bilberries

Serves 4

Florence Fennel 100g
Fennel Pollen Tops 35g
Spinach 50g
Water 85ml
Stock Syrup 85g
Skyr 100g
Wild Bilberries 80g

1. Freeze the green parts of the fennel. Blanch and refresh the spinach.

2. Transfer the frozen fennel and the pollen tops, spinach, water and syrup to a blender and blitz until smooth. Pass through a fine sieve.

3. Transfer to a shallow tray and freeze, whisking regularly to avoid lumps.

To Serve: Place the wild bilberries in the bottom of a bowl, add some skyr and finish with the granita.

Chapter VII

Japanese Menu

Generous Present Moment[9]

---

9 This title for this chapter is inspired by the work of neuroscientist, Dr Joe Dispenza.

The inspiration for this menu lies in both Japan and my family. In 2019, I visited Kyoto, Tokyo, Hakone, Ozaka, Hiroshima as well as Makurasaki, which is well known for its Katsoubshi production, the mainstay of Dashi. From a food and cultural perspective this trip was mind blowing, but it was made all the more special because I was accompanied by my son, Kenneth and my grandson Nathan. The act of spending time with the people you love is something that most people take for granted. I am not one of them. Every day I know I am blessed. But, this was not always the case; for many years I did not have a relationship with anyone in my family, and it took a considerable amount of time to heal the hurt and devastation this 'lost time' caused. However, time cannot be recaptured, it is gone forever and my mistakes cannot be 'undone'. I cannot change my past. So, now I live in the 'generous present moment', with a sense of immense gratitude and love for every waking moment that I get to spend with them. My experience in Japan enabled me to develop my relationship with both Kenneth and Nathan further, and for that I am eternally grateful.

While most Japanese people live in overpopulated cities that are commercially driven, high energy and full of hustle and bustle, this chapter celebrates my stay in a Buddhist Temple in Koyasan, near Kyoto, where we experienced a more traditional way of life, as well as the delicate, serene dishes of a form of cuisine referred to as Shojin Ryori.

Set in the dense forests of the Kii Mountains, the three sacred sites of Yoshino and Omine, Kumano Sanzan, and Koyasan (known as Kumano Kodo) have an intricate network of pilgrim routes that stretch over 200 miles, linking the ancient capital cities of Nara and Kyoto. My journey took me to Koyasan, Mount Kōya. This mountain range is regarded as one of the three most holy mountains in Japan.

This spectacular alpine mountain-scape of giant cedar and cypress trees is the setting for a complex tapestry of sacred spaces that celebrate the fusion of two of Japan's oldest and most influential spiritual traditions: the indigenous practice of Shintoism (nature-worship) and Buddhism (which originated in India, but was introduced to Japan via China and the Korean Peninsula in the 6th Century).[10]

Founded in 816, and consecrated in 819 by Kōbō-Daishi's (27th July, 774 – 22nd April 835), Koyasan is a collection of monasteries and temples that are surrounded by two spectacular mountain ranges that each have eight peaks resembling a lotus flower. It is also the site for Kongōbu-ji ('Temple of the Diamond Mountain Peak'), which is the central headquarters for Shingon Buddhism, as well as world famous Danjo Garan, a complex of 12 buildings, including Miedō (Great Portrait Hall), and a series of magnificent pagodas, shrines and religious buildings.

Kōbō-Daishi travelled to China in 804 where he was ordained as a Master of Shingon Buddhism. As a mountain ascetic and scholar he eventually became one of Japan's most revered saints.

According to legend when he was leaving China, Kōbō-Daishi prayed for guidance as to where to build his training centre. He threw a Sanko (a ceremonial tool) into the air vowing to set up his sanctuary wherever it landed. Kōbō-Daishi travelled widely looking for a place to establish his school. He searched everywhere for the Sanko, and when he arrived in the Kii mountains he stumbled upon a hunter with a spear and two dogs. Kōbō-Daishi followed the dogs across the Kino River, where he was greeted by a woman who was the master of Mount Koya. She guided him to find his Sanko hanging from a pine tree, and thus Kōbō-Daishi founded his temple in 816.[11]

It was here that he felt the 'cosmic Buddha energy', and thus he established Koyasan, which he referred to as 'hosshin no sato': the home of awakening faith.[12]

---

10 Buddhism dates back to over 2,500 years ago and was founded by Buddha Shakyamuni.

11 Story's source: https://www.fudouin.or.jp/english_koyasan.html

12 Source: *Temple Sojiin. 648-0211 Wakayama. Koyasan.* 143. JAPAN and temple video: https://www.youtube.com/watch?v=HKT43vP-B-A&t=5s

Koyasan is a centre for active devotion. It is a place filled with vibrancy and history, saffron robed monks with conical straw hats, prayer sticks, chanting and ritualistic fire ceremonies to burn away the root of all suffering. It is also a place of great art, where myth, architecture and spirituality combine to create an experience that I will never forget.

During our stay in Koyasan we stayed with monks in an Oubo (temple open to lay people). One evening, while awaiting our evening meal, I pondered my previous evening's visit to Kōbō-Daishi's mausoleum at the site of Okunoin, where it is believed that Kobo Daishi is not actually dead, but rests in eternal meditation as he awaits Miroku Nyorai (Maihrea), the Buddha of the Future.

It was dusk. The night was drawing in and I could smell the dampness of mist beginning to penetrate the forest. It was with both a sense of trepidation and apprehension that I ventured toward what was to become an unexpected encounter with 'the void'.

The site of Okunoin is the largest cemetery in Japan. A 2km lantern-lit pathway leading to the mausoleum illuminates thousands of tombs filled with ashes of the dead awaiting to be brought back to life when Kōbō-Daishi is reborn. Made of a cool dove-grey stone, the lanterns are inscribed with symbols and Japanese characters that take on the life and energy of the other-world. As soon as darkness descends, the lights, in the shape of different phases of the moon, penetrate deep into the dense forest-scape. As I followed the path into the woods it felt as if the forest was closing in. Fern-lace stone shapes framed by a tree-lined horizon of mist set the scene for the cold fear that began to seize my body. Covered in mottled dark green and yellow moss, the tombs flirt with elusive darting shadows that belong to the dark night sky. It took all my will to continue this noble journey through towering umbrella pine and hemlock trees. It was as if I was walking to the end of the world. Each tomb I passed commanded my attention.

I felt weak and vulnerable, and yet a mysterious expectation filled my heart just at the point when the scent of fallen pine needles and incense arrested my senses. It felt as if an indescribable presence penetrated the suffering hidden beneath countless layers of scarred memories.

Somehow, the foreboding stillness that emanated from the cold earth beneath my feet began to consume my attention. As I looked toward the shadows between the trees I saw multiple images of myself, bouncing back and forth on shafts of dew drop light. And then, a darkness erupted so forcefully before me that I could not move. I was compelled to gaze deeply into the void; into the emptiness that I had been running away from all my life. Yet, instead of being frozen by fear, my mind relaxed into a thousand fragments and, all at once, I felt the cravings release.

The darkness came closer and closer and I held out my hand, but I could not see it.

Yet, I could feel it.

I sensed it.

I drew a deep breath from the very centre of my being, and as I exhaled, the darkened mist lifted as I stepped 'out of time' into the unknown.

The path before me now rested at the entrance to the Torodo Hall of Worship, where 10,000 lanterns burn in perpetuity.[13]

---

13 I was told by a monk that two of these lanterns have been burning for over 900 years.

Back in my Shukubo, my thoughts were interrupted by a monk who invited me through delicate sliding doors (fusuma) to a room with a beautiful tatami floor and a traditional lacquered table of fresh and colourful cuisine. I was in awe of this quiet, soulful place, where Buddhist monks consider time spent cooking as important as formal meditation.

Over the course of my stay I learnt a lot about the art of Shojin Ryori and, in so doing, about myself.

Shojin Ryori 精進料理 was introduced to Kyōto monasteries in the 7th and 8th centuries via China and the Korean Peninsula. It was, however, the founder of the Sōtō sect of Zen Buddhism, Dōgen Zenji, and his teachings of *Tenzo Kyōkun* (*Instructions for the Cook*), that led to the proliferation of this practice throughout Japan.[14] The art of Shojin Ryori cuisine is now embedded in Japanese cultural and religious practice. It follows the practice of *Five Cooking Rules* (raw, boil, grill, fry and steam); the *Five Tastes* (sweet, sour, salty, bitter, and umami), and the *Five Colours* (white, yellow, red, blue and black). In addition, Shojin Ryori avoids strong flavoured ingredients, including garlic, onions, scallions, chives and leeks, due to their stimulating effect on the physical body.

> Shōjin food is seasonal, local and authentic (made with natural non-industrial ingredients). It consists of vegetables, grains, beans, sesame seeds, nuts, mush- rooms, fruits, wild herbs, seaweed, roots, agar, kudzu and dried or fermented foods. The seasonings to bring out the flavors of vegetables are made with konbu, sugar, salt, vinegar, miso, soy sauce, and saké. At the heart of shōjin, and indeed most Japanese cooking, is "one soup, one dish" (ichijuu issai 一汁 一菜). Rice and tsukemono (pickles) are also served, but are taken for granted and not counted in the phrase. This is also the essential Zen meal, which uses four nested bowls. Simple, yet profound.[15]

This minimalist, yet visually appealing cuisine, enables us to re-connect mindfully to the nature of the food being served.

Master of Shōjin Ryjoi, Tanahashi Toshio offers us a definition:

> '... shojin" consists of two characters —sho 精, to "purify," and jin 進, the word for "advance." In other words, "purifying the heart with real food enables us to move toward peace and clarity." Ryori 料理 commonly is translated as "cooking," but on a deeper and broader level the characters also mean "measuring truth."'[16]

Shojin Ryori is more than a method of food preparation, or vegetarian cuisine. It is an expression of ahimsa, or non-violence (hence the vegetarian emphasis); a daily commitment to cultivating integrity and wisdom, as well an act of contemplation of the universe through meditation and mindful cooking practices. The spirit of Shojin Ryori permeates every aspect of temple dining. The *'way'* of this sacred food experience is one of grace, with simple aesthetics and high ideals that are inspired by reflections upon the very nature of life itself, combined with a deep appreciation of our natural environment.

The emphasis upon nature and using seasonal produce is an opportunity to reflect on one of the core features of Buddhist philosophy: the teachings of impermanence; that all of life is transient and just like the seasons, everything goes through the cycle of change, birth, decay and rebirth.

When reflecting upon impermanence, the seasons and nature's wisdom through Buddhist thought we eventually stumble upon the teaching of attachment; our adherence to worldly constructs of reality that keep us in a state of suffering and, from a Buddhist point of view, stuck in the cycle of karma and rebirth.

---

14 Source: Toshio Tanahashi: SHOJIN Cuisine Master / Founder of ZECOOW Culinary Institute: <u>https://www.zecoow.com</u>

15 Shojinn Pamphlet in English: See: <u>www.zecoow.com.</u>

16 Source: SHOJIN Cuisine Master / Founder of ZECOOW Culinary Institute, Tanahashi Toshio, Ota Atsuko, Lucinda Cowing, John Einarsen.

Importantly, the teaching of non-attachment is evident in the preparation and presentation of the Shojin Ryori. By offering food that is as close to nature as possible, in its simplicity and uncomplicated state, the chef, cook or monk invites us to abandon preconceived notions of 'good' and 'bad', of preferences for taste and indulgence, and instead offers an opportunity to engage with the essence of the food itself.

In so doing, when we follow the 'way' of Shojin Ryori, we are encouraged to feel gratitude in the ordinary, to release the trappings of the material world as we engage in peaceful contemplation.

Here, it is important to consider that every aspect of food preparation is just as important as the dining experience. Plants are grown using traditional methods, with careful consideration to moon cycles and seasonal shifts. Herbs and plants are harvested with care and reverence, reminding us of our dependence on the life-force that the plants, earth, air, water and soil provide. In the kitchen, every part of the vegetable is prepared in meditation, with love and compassion.

The décor for the Shojin Ryori experience should be as tranquil and inviting as the food itself. Even the act of creating space for sharing food is regarded as an opportunity to pause from a world of suffering, and to be thankful for all that we are blessed with.

Importantly, the air of ceremony that is pervasive throughout the Son Ryroi dining experience is merely an extension of a monk's daily activity. For them, enlightenment is in practice.

'The first Shojin Ryori meal I had at the Shukubo, was remarkable:'

I gazed at the simple dish before me. Instead of jumping in to taste, I considered the various ingredients: shiitake mushrooms, limes, sesame tofu (gomadofu), green beans, rice and burdock, ginger, cucumber pickled in salted rice bran, and fig simmered with grape tapioca. Such simple food, and yet it was one of the most beautiful meals I had ever experienced.

It was during this meal that I made a commitment to explore bringing mindfulness into my own cooking and to explore deeper the quality of each ingredient. I had for many years followed the philosophy of 'let food speak for itself', but now I was mesmerised by the idea that a meal can be a practice of contemplation of the very nature of the universe, a celebration of being at 'one' with all things, and a vehicle for self-realisation.

When experiencing the essence of Shojin Ryori, I found myself catching a small glimpse of my true essence, one untainted by my past and unaffected by my trauma. That evening, while partaking in Shojin Ryori, there was no past or future, just the eternal, generous present moment.

Each mouthful was a taste of life itself, and each scent a reminder of our connection to the earth's abundance. Such seasonal freshness stirred such an aliveness within my body that I was moved to the point of tearful joy. The beauty of each dish aroused such a serene sense of gratitude that elevated every aspect of my being to a state of pure bliss. It was during these moments that I discovered that the true nature of cooking was to experience food by '*being it,*' rather than judging it by preconceived notions or cultural expectations. Eating Shojin Ryori was an opportunity to engage with food as part of a healing journey, as each ingredient was prepared with such love and kindness that it nourished more than my body; it nurtured my soul in a way that could not be explained in words. It can *only* be experienced. When I was eating I had everything in that moment that I needed. I was in tune, connected and in flow with the energy and elegance of this beautiful moment.

After the meal had finished, I sat for a while in pure meditative gratitude and a sense of peace and acceptance flowed gently through my body-mind and, all at once, I was free.

I now know that I cannot avoid my suffering, nor can I hold on to happiness; indeed both experiences are fleeting exchanges of the same transient form. We can taste, yet soon the food will be gone, and all we are left with is the memory, impression and essence of the ingredients. When we assimilate these vegetables the very energy of the plants fill our being with vitality and energy and their signature becomes ours, just for a while... but, that too will pass.

While eating Shojin Ryori I realised that I was part of a larger cycle of life and death, one that I cannot control or resist.

In the stark light of day, when analysed with an enquiring mind, this assertion may appear bleak. But, in some strange way it gave me hope. It released me from the incessant searching for answers and forgiveness.

Buddhists approach the world with compassion, patience and joy; emotions that I have struggled with all my life.

Cooking, however, brings me a sense of peace and acceptance, so I really relate to the path of Shojin Ryori.

There is a sense that the temple food served in Koyasan is from the heart, filled with mindful moments of magic that offer the weary traveller in all of us an opportunity to find stillness in the chaos of everyday life.

It is my desire that the dishes in this chapter will offer you an opportunity to do so as well.

Japanese Menu

Generous Present Moment

Citrus and Seaweed

Mushroom Broth

Koji Rice and Pumpkin Seed Cake with Fermented Pumpkin Juice

Peas, Beans and Hazelnuts

Fig Leaf Sorbet and Salted Fig

This menu invites you to follow the 'Way of Shojin Ryori'.

When we take time to meditate before dining it provides us with an opportunity to deepen our awareness of the subtle flavours, colours, character, texture and scent of each meal, thus stimulating taste receptors, digestive processes, and importantly, a deeper appreciation of the very nature of life itself.

Create the extraordinary out of the ordinary.

Citus and Seaweed

Serves 4

Pink Grapefruit Segments 4

Lemon Segments 4

Kumquats 4

Orange segments 4

Sugar 10g

Water 10ml

Seaweed 50g

Sunflower Oil 20g

1. Bring oil to 65°C. Add dried seaweed and leave to infuse overnight.

2. Blend the oil and seaweed mixture and strain through a fine sieve (or muslin cloth).

3. To make stock syrup: bring the sugar and water to the boil. Remove from the heat and add the kumquats to the warm syrup. Allow to cool and store in the refrigerator.

4. Check that there are no pips in the segments of the orange, grapefruit and lemon.

5. Add the lemon segments to the stock syrup and leave for two to three hours.

To Serve: Drain all the fruits. Lightly dress with seaweed oil and arrange in a suitable dish.

Note: You can experiment with almost any fruit you wish.

Mushroom Broth

Serves 4

Dried Shiitake Mushrooms
20g

Enokitake (Enoki)
Mushrooms 10g

Vegetable Stock 1 litre

White Miso Paste
1 tablespoon

Soy Sauce 2 tablespoons

Mirin 1 tablespoon

Sake 1 tablespoon

Sesame Seeds 1 teaspoon

Rice Noodles 10g

Coriander, a few sprigs

Ginger 5g

1. Crush garlic with the back of your knife, slice peeled ginger and place in a saucepan. Add vegetable stock, dried mushrooms, miso, soy sauce, mirin and sake. Bring to the boil and simmer for five minutes.

2. Leave to cool. When cool, strain through a fine sieve or muslin.

3. Cook the noodles in boiling salted water. Ensure that they retain a bite. Drain and leave in a little water.

4. Reheat the broth.

5. Divide the noodles and enokitake mushrooms between the bowls.

To Serve: Pour the broth over the noodles and enokitake mushrooms and garnish with chopped coriander.

Koji Rice and Pumpkin Seed Cake with Fermented Pumpkin Juice

Serves 4

Long Grain Rice 400g
Koji 1 teaspoon
Pumpkin Seeds 150g
Sea Salt 2g
Pumpkin Juice (fermented) 50g (see page 140)

1. Wash the rice in cold running water and soak in fresh cold water for 6 hours.

2. Steam rice until cooked (30 minutes), but not overcooked.

3. Add salted pumpkin seeds.

4. Cool to 30°C and inoculate with koji spores. Transfer to a suitable tray (Gastronome).

5. Cover with a chemical-free, clean tea-towel and place in a dark humid environment for 48 hours. Check every 12 hours.

6. It is ready when a wispy white membrane has formed around the rice.

To Serve: Lightly caramelise the top of the cake with a blow torch, or under a hot grill. Divide into portions. Brush with miso and serve with fermented pumpkin juice (see Fermentation section).

Peas, Beans and Hazelnuts

Serves 4

Vegetable Stock 200ml
Dried Porcini 8g
Juniper Berries 5g
Broad Beans 100g
Fresh Peas 10g
Pineapple Weed (dried) 10g
Hazelnuts 8g
Green Tea Oil
(see page 146)
Butter 10g

1. Bring the stock to the boil. Add the dried mushrooms, pineapple weed, juniper berries and gooseberries. Leave to infuse overnight.

2. Boil a little water and add the butter and blend with an immersion blender to an emulsion.

3. Add shelled and peeled broad beans and peas to the emulsion and heat gently.

To Serve: Divide the broad bean mixture into 4 warm bowls and add the hot infusion split with green tea oil, then finish with grated hazelnuts. Garnish with fresh pineapple weed heads and edible flowers.

Fig Leaf Sorbet and Salted Fig

In addition to being inspired by my experience in Koyasan, this dessert is influenced also by street food popular in Minooear Osaka. It is a take on a maple leaf (using instead a fig leaf) tempura.

Serves 4

Fig Leaves 700g
Water 800g
Sugar 500g
Glucose 120g
Agar Agar 3g
Sunflower Oil 20ml
Figs 4

1. Fig leaf infusion: Bring the water and sugar to the boil. Pour over 500g of fig leaves.

2. Cover with cling film and infuse for 1 week in the refrigerator.

3. Strain through a sieve.

4. Salted figs: Weigh the figs. Cut in half and add 2% sea salt. Place in a Kilner jar with a weight on top and ferment for 5 to 7 days at room temperature.

5. Remove the figs and reduce the residual juice and use to glaze.

6. Sorbet: Heat the fig infusion. Add the glucose and whisk in the agar and place in an ice-cream machine (or in a suitable container) and freeze, ensuring that you scrape it every 2 hours until you achieve the desired result.

To Serve: Place a generous spoonful of sorbet into a bowl. Put a salted (glazed) fig on top and finish with a deep fried (190°C) fig leaf.

Note: The infusion, sorbet and salted figs can be prepared a week in advance with the exception of the deep fried fig leaf.

Chapter VIII

Additional Recipes

FERMENTED PRODUCTS

I tend to use the same technique for most of my ferments by combining 2% salt to the weight of the product. For example, take one kilo of peeled pumpkin and cut into even sized pieces. Add 20 grams of sea salt. Gently massage the salt into the pumpkin (osmosis). Place ingredients into a Kilner jar or vacuum pack. Leave at room temperature for 3 to 5 weeks. The result is quite amazing. On the one hand, you have the sweetness of the pumpkin and on the other, you get the wonderful sourness from the fermentation process. The juice can be used in dressings, marinades and as sauce. The pumpkin flesh can be lightly roasted and served as a vegetable or puréed, dehydrated and served as crisps. I am trying constantly to come up with interesting types of ferments ranging from fermented pumpkin guts to honey. Similarly, take a kilo of shredded cabbage and add 2% salt. In a few weeks you have sauerkraut.

I am not an expert in the making of traditional Japanese ferments, which is a staple part of Japan's cuisine, but I have made my own version of Katsoubushi with line caught Irish tuna. Feeling inspired with the relative success of my Katsoubushi, which is a crucial part of Dashi (as well as kombu), I am currently working on both a Musselbushi and an Oysterbushi, both of which are harvested on the west coast of Ireland. They are nice and plump with a good salinity, making them the perfect candidate for this particular process of curing, smoking, cooking, drying and inoculation.

Method

Use a 60% salt to 40% sugar ratio and then a thirty percent ratio of this mixture to the weight of the mussels and oysters sprinkled over them and cured overnight. The salt is made from the oyster juice, which is dehydrated, producing an exceptional sea salt (a technique I learned while staging at Maaemo). This is a wonderful way of making sure you utilise all the Oyster. They are then cold smoked for twelve hours, cooked sous vide at 75°C for 45 minutes. They are then dehydrated at 30°C, until extremely hard (usually 1 week). Finally, they are sprayed with aspergillus glaucus (see note below), which is traditionally used in the making of Katsoubushi. It is incubated at 28°C and 65% humidity for over a week. The mould is quite slow to take hold. However, once it grows, the flavour of the oyster is completely transformed.

However, while the mussels did not work this time, I will continue to experiment with fermentation. The reason I am sharing this recipe with you is to show you how you can experiment with local produce (contact us and let us know how you get on).

See The Noma Guide to Fermentation on the construction of a fermentation chamber. Noma holds three-Michelin stars and in 2021 came first in the World's 50 Best Restaurants.

All of this sounds quite complicated, but once you delve into the amazing world of fermentation you will become totally addicted, as I am. I started off making sauerkraut and kimchi (see Sandor Ellix Katz: The Art of Fermentation, 2012) and now I am hooked.

The excellent book Koji Alchemy: *Rediscovering the Magic of Mold-Based Fermentation* by Rich Shih and Jeremy Umansky (2020) is 'the manual' to using koji.

Umeboshi

My father passed away fifteen years ago and sadly the garden no longer produces fruit and vegetables. However, the plum tree remains and still bears fruit, so every year I make umeboshi. In Japan, umeboshi is traditionally made with green, sour ume plums, which are salted, fermented and dried in the sun.

I use regular plums:

Take 1kg of plums, cut in half, remove the stone, weigh them and add 2% salt. You can then transfer the salted plums to a Kilner jar, put a weight on top (or vacuum pack) and store at room temperature for around two weeks. Remove the plums and dehydrate at 55°C for about 8 hours to semi-dry, or overnight in a low oven at the same temperature. The result is a salty, sour intense plum. Do not discard the liquid, as it can be used in salad dressings with goat's cheese. It is also amazing with pork or duck. You can purée the umeboshi and store in a sterilised jar, or leave whole. This process can also be applied to cherries, figs, gooseberries and apricots.

Kimchi

In essence, kimchi is a spicy sauerkraut, where the transformative process of fermentation turns the sugar in the vegetables into lactic acid, creating an environment in which complex flavours emerge. However, if you add chilli and fish sauce to this concoction, you can create a really funky kraut that does not disappoint.

Kimchi is hugely versatile and can be used on its own, part of a salad, or added to soups, noodles, pancakes, omelettes, or burgers.

Serves 8-10

Carrots Peelings 400g
Cabbage Trim 400g
Spring Onion 200g
Garlic 2 cloves (crushed)
Ginger 4cm piece, peeled and finely diced.
Sugar 10g
Fish Sauce 2 teaspoons
Korean Chilli 2 teaspoons
Shrimp paste 1 teaspoons (optional)
Sea Salt 20g (2%)

1. Combine all the vegetables in a large bowl.
2. Weigh the vegetables and add 2% salt and mix well.
3. Cover with a clean cloth and leave for 2 to 3 hours.
4. Mix the garlic, shrimp paste, chilli, fish sauce and ginger to a paste.
5. Add vegetables and mix well.
6. Pack into a sterilised 1 litre Kilner jar and ferment at room temperature for 7 to 10 days. Store away from sunlight.
7. This can then be stored in the refrigerator for up to three months.

Note: After Christmas, I usually make brussels sprout kimchi. Just replace the peelings with 800g of brussels sprouts (quartered). You can also use the stalks, leaves of cauliflower, broccoli, etc. The possibilities are endless.

Fermented Honey

Organic Honey 250g
Water 1 litre
Dried Meadowsweet 75g

1. Dissolve the honey in lukewarm water. Pour into a sterilised container and cover with a muslin cloth, secure with an elastic band or twine. Leave in a warm environment (room temperature) for seven days, stirring regularly.

2. Add the dried meadowsweet, cover with an airtight lid and water lock. Leave in a cool dark environment for twelve weeks.

3. To serve: strain through muslin cloth and serve.

Note: I dry the meadowsweet on my kitchen window with the sun shining through. It is perfect after two days. Alternatively, you could place it on a sheet of newspaper and dry in the hot-press/airing cupboard.

Chicken Stock

Most chicken stocks tend to use chicken carcasses, onion, celery, carrot, etc. What I am trying to achieve here is to maximise the chicken flavour by limiting the amount of aromatics to onion, apple for a little acidity and some thyme. The result is an excellent chicken stock.

Makes about 2 litres

Chicken Wings 3kg
Onion 1
Apples 1
Thyme – a small sprig
Water 4 litres

1. Brown chicken wings in a hot oven 180°C.

2. Drain wings in a colander.

3. Place wings, cold water, apple and thyme in a pan.

4. Bring to a simmer and skim all the fat from the surface.

5. Continue to simmer gently and skim regularly for 3 hours approx.

6. Chill, stock and refrigerate overnight.

7. Remove all the solidified fat from the surface.

8. Bring to a simmer and pass through a sieve or muslin cloth.

9. Use as required.

Seaweed and Salt Dough

Plain Flour 300g
Fine Sea Salt 200g
Egg Whites 60g
Water 160g
Dried Seaweed (finely chopped) 10g

1. Prepare dough by combining all the dry ingredients in a bowl, add egg white and slowly add the water until you achieve a firm dough.
2. Wrap in cling film and refrigerate for hours.
3. Roll the dough to about 3cm in thickness.
4. Use as required.

FLAVOURED OILS

For herbs to provide us with flavour, we need to liberate the essence of the plants.

Depending on the type of herb, there are different techniques: cold or hot extraction. For example, some herbs such as thyme, heather and spring onion require heat to capture their essence. Softer herbs such as lemon verbena, chives, dill, parsley, lovage, etc., need to be infused by putting the herbs in oil for a few days.

Spring Onion Oil (scallion)

Onion Tops 250g
Rapeseed Oil 250g

1. Thermomix at 80°C for 8 minutes at speed 4.
2. Then speed 10 for 3 minutes, strain through a muslin cloth.
3. Store in a cool place.
4. Alternatively, heat oil to same temperature and pour over the onion tops and blend.

Leek Oil

Leek Green Part 250g
Sunflower Oil 500ml

Method: Same as Scallion Oil.

Wild Garlic Oil

Wild Garlic 250g
Sunflower Oil 500ml

Method: Same as Scallion Oil.

Nettle Oil

Nettles 450g
Sunflower Oil 900ml

1. Blanch the nettles in boiling salted water for 10 seconds.
2. Refresh in iced water.
3. Squeeze out any excess water.
4. Blend the nettles and oil together.
5. Store in a cool place overnight.
6. Strain through muslin cloth and use.

Dill Oil

Dill 250g
Sunflower Oil 500ml

1. Place the dill and oil into a Kilner jar or bottle and infuse for 5 to 7 days.
2. Strain and use as required.

Lemon Verbena Oil

Lemon Verbena 50g
Sunflower Oil 300ml

Method: Same as Dill Oil.

Green Tea Oil

Green Tea Leaves 500g
Sunflower Oil 1000ml

1. Place oil and tea leaves into a vacuum bag, seal and cook sous vide at 60°C for 8 hours.
2. Alternatively, place oil and tea leaves in a pan cover and transfer to an oven at 60°C for the same time.
3. Strain the oil and decant into a bottle, store in a cool place.

Kelp/Seaweed Oil

Kelp 500g
Sunflower Oil 1000ml

1. Dehydrate the kelp/seaweed in a dehydrator or an oven at 60°C until completely dry, usually 6 to 8 hours.
2. Place oil and seaweed into a vacuum bag, seal and cook sous vide at 60°C for 8 hours. Alternatively, place oil and seaweed in a pan cover and transfer to an oven at 60°C for the same time.
3. Strain the oil and decant into a bottle, store in a cool place.

Crispy Shallots and Oil

Shallots 1kg
Sunflower Oil 2000ml

1. Thinly slice the shallots.

2. Transfer the oil to a suitable pan and add the sliced shallots, always starting with cold oil and continually stirring the shallots.

3. After about 20 minutes the shallots should begin to crisp up.

4. Remove the shallots with a slotted spoon and drain on kitchen paper.

5. Season with salt and use as required.

6. Strain the oil and re-use again or decant into a bottle and use to dress dishes. It also makes a really nice shallot flavoured mayonnaise.

Heather Oil

Heather 500g
Sunflower Oil 500ml

Method: Same as Kelp Oil.

Lobster Oil

Lobster Shells 1
Sunflower Oil 300g

1. Wash the lobster shell including the head in cold water.

2. Heat oil in a pan and add dried crushed carcass.

3. Place the oil and shells into a suitable dish and roast at 120°C for 90 minutes. Skim any impurities that rise to the surface. Leave to infuse for ninety minutes.

4. Strain through a sieve/muslin cloth and store in the refrigerator.

Note: Crab, shrimp or prawns can also be used. These oils add another layer of flavour to many dishes. Indeed, I often make mayonnaise using the lobster oil.

PICKLES

Basic Pickle

Vinegar 1000ml
Water 2000ml
Sugar 900ml

1. Combine all the ingredients and bring to the boil.
2. Strain into a clean jar and use as required.

Rose-hip Petals
Cherry Blossoms
Seaweed
Gooseberries
Rhubarb
Shallots
Beetroot, Carrot, etc.
Pine shoots
Elderflowers

1. Bring the vinegar, sugar and water to the boil.
2. Make sure that the sugar has dissolved.
3. Place any of the above ingredients in a sterilised Kilner jar and pour over the warm liquid.
4. Seal and store.
5. Use as required.

Note: The above list can be expanded by including almost any ingredient such as onion or shallot and you also have a flavoured vinegar.

INFUSIONS | JUICES | NON ALCOHOLIC DRINKS

Apple and Parsley

Fresh Apple Juice 1 litre
Flat Parsley 500g

1. Juice the apples and the parsley separately.
2. Combine both juices, chill and serve.

Apple, Cucumber and Seaweed Oil

Attyflin Apple Juice 1 litre
Cucumber 1
Seaweed Oil – a few drops

1. Juice the cucumber and add to the apple juice.
2. Chill and serve in a suitable glass garnished with mint and seaweed oil.

Red Pepper and Lettuce

Red Peppers (to make 1 litre juice)

Butterhead Lettuce (to make 200ml juice)

Sea Salt 5g

1. Char the peppers on a naked flame until totally blackened.
2. Transfer the peppers to a bowl and cover with cling film.
3. By covering, it creates steam making it easier to remove the charred skin.
4. Wash off the charred skin and remove the seeds.
5. Juice the peppers and put aside.
6. Juice some butterhead lettuce.
7. Combine both juices, add salt, stir and pass through a muslin cloth.
8. Served chilled.

Grapes, Fennel and Honey

Green Grapes 1kg

Florence Fennel 1 head

Honey to taste

1. Juice the grapes and fennel separately.
2. Combine the juices and add honey to taste.
3. Chill and serve in a cocktail glass.

Hyssop Tea

Hyssop has been used for centuries and is known to have antiseptic qualities. It can be bitter and has a really nice mint element to it that is complemented by floral notes that are wonderfully aromatic.

Water 350ml

Dried Hyssop (Agastache foeniculum) leaves 1 tablespoon

Honey as required

1. Bring water to the boil.
2. Pour the water over the hyssop leaves.
3. Add honey.

Note: this can also be served cold.

Pineapple Weed Tea

I first came across this wonderful wildflower while staging at Maaemo in Oslo. Since then, I have been constantly looking for it. The distinctive feature of this wild plant is that it smells and tastes like pineapple. Indeed, the young leaves are also excellent in salads.

Water 350ml

Dried Pineapple Weed (Matricaria discoidea) 400g (buds and stalks)

1. Bring water to the boil.

2. Pour the water over the pineapple weed.

3. Cover and leave to infuse for five to six hours.

4. Strain and chill.

Elderflower Soda

The elder (Sambucus nigra) was once held to be an unlucky tree in Ireland. According to Irish folklore, there are three signs of a cursed or abandoned place: the elder, the nettle and the corncrake. The tree was also seen as a symbol of grief because of its connection with death.

Water 5 litres

Elderflowers 50g

Sugar 250g

1. Bring water and sugar to the boil. Take off the heat and add elderflowers. Cover and allow to infuse for at least 1 hour.

2. Pass through a sieve/ muslin cloth.

3. Charge in a SodaStream and serve.

Elderflower Cordial

Elderflowers 40 clusters

Lemons 2 (unwaxed)

Caster Sugar 500g

Water 2 litres

Citric Acid 50g

1. Shake the flowers to remove any insects.

2. Bring the water to the boil.

3. Place sugar, lemon rind into a pan and add boiling water to dissolve the sugar.

4. Add citric acid and pour the syrup over the elderflowers.

5. Cover and infuse for two days.

6. Strain the cordial through a fine sieve/muslin cloth.

7. Bottle and store.

8. Dilute as required with sparkling water and serve.

KOMBUCHA

Kombucha is a fermented tea, traditionally made with green tea. It can also be made by substituting the tea with a sweetened herbal infusion, coffee, elderflower, etc. The finished product is a slightly soured effervescent drink. Once you start on the fermentation journey, the possibilities are endless. Scobies (short for 'symbiotic communities of bacteria and yeasts') can be purchased online and in health food shops.

Basic Green Tea Kombucha

Sugar 160g
Organic Green Tea Bags 8
Still Water 2 litres
Scoby 1

1. Boil 500 grams of water, add sugar to a plastic bowl/jug, add boiled water to dissolve sugar.
2. Add tea bags and infuse for 20 minutes.
3. Add remainder of cold water.
4. Make sure the liquid is cool before adding the scoby.
5. Strain into a sterilised Kilner jar. Add scoby
6. Cover with muslin cloth and secure with a rubber band.
7. Leave in a dark place for 7 days.
8. Bottle for another 3 days (2nd ferment).
9. Store in the refrigerator and serve chilled.

Note: At the 2nd ferment stage you can add fruits to flavour the drink.

Elderflower Kombucha

Caster Sugar 160g
Still Water 2 litres
Elderflower Blossoms
350g
Previous Kombucha 200g
Scoby – 1 that will cover at
least 25% of the surface.

1. Bring the water and sugar to the boil, constantly stirring to dissolve the sugar.
2. Place the blossoms into a heat proof container.
3. Pour the hot syrup over the blossoms.
4. Cool down and refrigerate overnight to infuse.
5. Strain through muslin cloth, pressing to extract all the liquid.
6. Add the 200g of previous kombucha and pour into a large Kilner jar.
7. Wearing gloves, place the scoby into the syrup.
8. Cover with muslin cloth and secure with string or an elastic band.
9. Leave in a warm dark place to ferment for 7 days.
10. Remove the scoby to a suitable container.
11. Strain kombucha, bottle it and leave to ferment for 3 days (2nd Ferment)
12. Store in the refrigerator and serve chilled.

Wild Rose Infusion

Water 1 litre
Rose Petals 300g
Caster Sugar 200g

1. Ensure rose petals are free from insects (use pastry brush to clean).
2. Bring water and sugar to the boil.
3. Ensure that the sugar is dissolved.
4. Allow to cool slightly and pour over the rose petals.
5. Keep in a sterilised container.

To Serve: Strain and use in desserts, ice-cream, sponges and pastries.

Index of Recipes